Secrets of

the

LOST
SYMBOL

ABOUT THE AUTHOR

A student of magic and the unexplained for more than thirty years and the author of more than a dozen books, including the award-winning *New Encyclopedia of the Occult*, John Michael Greer has earned a reputation as one of the most original writers in the occult field today. His background combines academic study in the history of ideas with training and initiation in several occult and Druid orders. He lives in the mountains of southern Oregon with his wife, Sara.

Secrets of the

the

LOST
SYMBOL

The Unauthorized Guide to
Secret Societies,
Hidden Symbols
& Mysticism

JOHN MICHAEL GREER

Llewellyn Publications
Woodbury, Minnesota

First Edition
First Printing, 2009

Cover art: background parchment © iStockphoto.com/Duncan Walker
    and wax seal © iStockphoto.com/Stefan Klein
Cover design by Kevin R. Brown
Project management by Tom Bilstad
Excerpted from *The New Encyclopedia of the Occult* (Llewellyn, 2003)
Llewellyn is a registered trademark of Llewellyn Worldwide, Ltd.

Library of Congress Cataloging-in-Publication Data
Greer, John Michael.
  Secrets of the lost symbol : the unauthorized guide to secret societies, hidden symbols & mysticism / by John Michael Greer.—1st ed.
    p. cm.
  Includes bibliographical references and index.
  ISBN 978-0-7387-2169-9
  1. Brown, Dan, 1964– Lost symbol—Encyclopedias. 2. Secret societies in literature. 3. Freemasonry in literature. 4. Symbolism in literature. I. Title.
  PS3552.R685434L6734 2009
  813'.54—dc22

2009046830

Llewellyn Worldwide does not participate in, endorse, or have any authority or responsibility concerning private business transactions between our authors and the public.

  All mail addressed to the author is forwarded but the publisher cannot, unless specifically instructed by the author, give out an address or phone number.

  Any Internet references contained in this work are current at publication time, but the publisher cannot guarantee that a specific location will continue to be maintained. Please refer to the publisher's website for links to authors' websites and other sources.

Llewellyn Publications
A Division of Llewellyn Worldwide, Ltd.
2143 Wooddale Drive, Dept. 978-0-7387-2169-9
Woodbury, Minnesota 55125-2989, U.S.A.
www.llewellyn.com

Printed in the United States of America

BOOKS BY JOHN MICHAEL GREER

Inside a Magical Lodge
(December 1998)

Monsters
(September 2001)

Sacred Geometry Oracle
(January 2002)

The New Encyclopedia of the Occult
(October 2003)

Encyclopedia of Natural Magic
(April 2005)

Atlantis
(October 2007)

The UFO Phenomenon
(March 2009)

INTRODUCTION

While the *The Lost Symbol* by Dan Brown may be a work of fiction, the author includes many elements of reality and truth in his book, especially occult lore. (The word "occult" merely means "hidden.") But when the lines between reality and fiction are blurred, especially in a mystery novel such as *The Lost Symbol*, just how much is really the truth, and what is merely fiction?

The Secrets of the Lost Symbol is here to aid in understanding the "occult" truth behind the hidden lore found in *The Lost Symbol*. Arranged as encyclopedic entries, this reference book is meant to supplement *The Lost Symbol*. (For those who haven't read the novel yet, there are no spoilers in this book!) As a bonus, some of the occult elements hinted at in *The Lost Symbol* can be found here, too, which will add an even deeper meaning to the "occult" and "open" truths used in Dan Brown's latest novel.

Abramelin the Mage, The Sacred Magic of: A grimoire preserved in a single eighteenth-century copy in the Bibliotheque de l'Arsenal in Paris. Written in French, it claims to be a translation of a Hebrew original dating from 1458, although scholars have cast doubt on this claim.

According to the long preface, it represents the teachings of a Jewish magician named Abramelin, passed on by him to his student Abraham, and by the latter to his son Lamech. These teachings, which Abraham describes as the only valid magical system in the world, require the student to devote six months of prayer, repentance, and ritual to obtain the "Knowledge and Conversation of the Holy Guardian Angel." After this accomplishment, the student gains the power to command evil spirits through talismans composed of letter combinations.

The Sacred Magic was rediscovered in the late 1890s by Golden Dawn founder Samuel Mathers (1854–1918), and Mathers' English translation was published in 1898. It has had a major impact on magical thinking ever since, especially through its influence on Aleister Crowley (1875–1947), who used it as the template for much of his own understanding of magic. To this day the idea that magic is or should be directed toward the knowledge and contemplation of one's Holy Guardian Angel—a concept not found outside this work in older sources—is commonplace in magical writings.

The book itself, however, developed a sinister reputation among occultists in the early part of this century. Dire accidents and mental imbalance were held to have befallen many of those who owned a copy of the original printing, or who tried to use the talismans contained in it.

adept: (from Latin *adeptus*, "skillful") In most systems of Western occult thought, a title or grade used for (and by) advanced students of magic, alchemy, and other occult subjects. In alchemical tradition, only those capable of making the Philosopher's Stone were considered adepts. In modern ceremonial magic, similarly, the title is usually reserved for those who have penetrated the Veil of the Sanctuary and entered into contact with their Higher Genius or Holy Guardian Angel.

Some confusion has been caused over the years by the use of "adept" in occult lodges as a grade of initiation, since those who have passed through a given grade ritual may or may not have attained the spiritual experience that grade represents. As a result, the term has passed out of use in many parts of the magical community, except as a label for these grades.

Adonai: (Hebrew ADNI, "Lord") One of the traditional Hebrew names of God, usually assigned to the tenth Sephirah of the Tree of Life, Malkuth. In reading the Bible aloud in Jewish religious services, this name is used whenever the text gives YHVH, the Tetragrammaton, which is considered too sacred to vocalize.

Adonai was among the first of the Jewish divine names to be taken up by non-Jewish magicians, and appears frequently in classical magical texts such as the Graeco-Egyptian magical papyri. The relation of this name to the God of the Old Testament was sometimes remembered and sometimes completely forgotten; in some sources, Adonai or Adonaios is an angel, in others an independent divine being, and in still others an archon—that is, a power of ignorance or evil.

Adoptive Masonry: Any of several quasi-Masonic lodge systems for women, usually organized and run by male Freemasons. Many such systems came into existence in the eighteenth century, spurred by the success of the Mopses and other orders open to both genders. The

Grand Orient of France in 1774 organized these into a rite of three degrees called the Rite of Adoption.

In the United States, the Order of the Eastern Star is the most popular adoptive rite, although there are several others. None of these rites seems to have included much in the way of occult content, but adoptive lodges once played an important role in training women in initiatory ritual and lodge management—skills that were sometimes put to use in more explicitly magical contexts.

adytum: In ancient Greek and Roman religion, a shrine built into the basement level of a temple and used for ceremonies not open to the general public. The term has been used in several occult organizations, either as a synonym for "temple" or in a more metaphorical sense.

AGLA: A Cabalistic divine Name formed by notariqon from the Hebrew sentence *Ateh Gibor Le-olam, Adonai* ("Mighty art Thou forever, Lord"). It was much used in medieval ceremonial magic as a word giving power over demons.

Aiq beker: A method of Cabalistic number analysis, also known as the Cabala of Nine Chambers and theosophical reduction. It is based on the numerical values of the Hebrew letters. In Aiq beker, Aleph (which has a value of 1), Yod (with a value of 10), and Qoph (with a value of 100) all equal 1; Beth (2), Kaph (20), and Resh (200) all equal 2; Gimel (3), Lamed (30), and Shin (300) all equal 3, and so on up the alphabet to Teth (9), Tzaddi (90), and Tzaddi final (900), which all equal 9. Each of these groups of numbers is a "chamber," and the nonsense-words "Aiq beker" are simply what happens when a speaker of Hebrew pronounces the letters in the first two chambers, AIQ BKR. Aside from its use as a tool for gematria, Aiq beker has also been put to use as the basis for ciphers and other methods of secret communication.

Akhenaten: Egyptian pharaoh, reigned c. 1370–c. 1353 BCE. The discovery of Akhenaten's existence was one of the major surprises of nineteenth-century Egyptology. Starting in the 1840s, surveys of the Amarna plateau—a desolate site across the Nile from the ancient city of Hermopolis—turned up carvings of figures worshipping a sun-disk. The archeologists noted with surprise that the style of these carvings violated many of the standard principles of ancient Egyptian art, and that the names and faces of the figures had been systematically erased some time after they were originally carved. Interest in these so-called "disk worshippers" led to a series of digs at Amarna, to the discovery of a lost city and a forgotten pharaoh, and to controversies that have yet to be settled.

Much of the confusion around Akhenaten is a product of modern interpretations heavy with bias. Nineteenth-century Egyptologists such as William Flinders Petrie projected their own Christian beliefs onto Akhenaten, and presented a glorified and largely inaccurate picture of his reign and his ideas. In the twentieth century, people ranging from the neo-Nazi theorist Savitri Devi to certain modern Rosicrucian figures have co-opted Akhenaten for their own points of view; *SEE* ANCIENT MYSTICAL ORDER ROSAE CRUCIS (AMORC). Ideas such as these are still current in many circles, and have done much to obscure the life of one of ancient Egypt's most complex figures.

Akhenaten was the second son of Amenhotep III, among the greatest kings of Egypt's Eighteenth Dynasty, and was originally named Amenhotep after his father. There may have been ill feeling between father and son, as the young Amenhotep—unlike his siblings—is not named or portrayed on his father's surviving monuments. Some modern researchers, noting some of the odder details of portraits of Akhenaten made during his reign, have suggested that he may have suffered from a serious hormonal disorder called Fröhlich's syndrome. Still, he became crown prince upon the death of his elder brother Thutmose, and ascended to the throne a few years later as Amenhotep IV.

Shortly after his coronation, according to an inscription that survives in fragmentary form, he proclaimed that the traditional gods and goddesses of Egypt were lifeless and powerless; the only true god was Aten, the disk of the sun. Over the next few years, he pushed through a religious revolution, abolishing the temples and priesthoods of all gods but his own, erasing the names of the old gods from monuments throughout Egypt, and changing his own name from Amenhotep, "Amun is satisfied," to Akhenaten, "Spirit of Aten."

In the first years of his reign, he built four massive temples for Aten in the capitol city of Thebes, and in the fifth year abandoned Thebes altogether and moved to the Amarna plateau to build a new city called Akhetaten, "Horizon of Aten." There he oversaw the construction of an immense temple to Aten and a lavish palace for himself, built and decorated in a new style that owed nothing to the traditional sacred geometries of classic Egyptian art and architecture.

Akhenaten was apparently the closest thing to a complete materialist that ancient Egypt ever produced. Mythic and symbolic modes of human experience passed him by completely. To other ancient Egyptians ,the sun could be seen as a hawk hovering in the air, a celestial boat, a lion-headed or cat-headed goddess, or the right eye of a god; on its way through the sky, it did battle against a celestial serpent, risked running aground in the shoals of heaven, and carried the spirits of the dead to paradise. To Akhenaten, none of this was true. The sun was a shining disk in the sky and nothing else, and its actions were limited to those that could be seen and measured with ordinary vision: rising, shining, nourishing plants, and so on. The gods of the temples, in turn, were nothing but dead statues. In place of the rich mythic texture of Egyptian religion, Akhenaten proclaimed his own teaching of the supremacy of Aten, the solar disk, as the one living god and source of all life. He was apparently a poet of some talent—an impressive hymn to Aten found in Amarna-period tombs is believed to have been written by the pharaoh himself—but his view of the world stopped at the edge of the visible.

The last years of his reign were troubled. The soaring taxes and forced labor needed for the pharaoh's massive building projects left Egypt in a state of economic crisis, and large parts of the Egyptian empire fell under the control of the expanding Hittite kingdom in the north. To make matters worse, epidemic disease swept the country. Many Egyptians felt that just as Egypt had abandoned the gods, the gods had abandoned Egypt. Akhenaten's death, in the seventeenth year of his reign, brought his religious revolution to a halt. Three short-lived successors—Smenkhare, the boy-king Tutankhamen, and Ay—tried to find middle ground, maintaining the cult of Aten while permitting the old temples to be reopened. None of the three left heirs, and on Ay's death the double crown of Egypt passed to Horemheb, the commander of the army. Horemheb has been made into a villain in many modern accounts of Akhenaten's reign and its aftermath. In reality, he was a shrewd realist who saw that cooperation between the military and the temple priesthoods was essential to Egypt's survival. His reign of twenty-five years restored Egypt to stability and prosperity, and laid the foundations for the successes of the Nineteenth Dynasty, founded by his adopted son and heir Rameses I. He cut taxes and reformed the court system to win popular support, and ensured the backing of the temple priesthoods by restoring the old temples to their original splendor and position in society. The complete termination of Akhenaten's religious revolution was an essential part of Horemheb's work. By the new pharaoh's command, the temples of Aten were systematically destroyed, and the city of Akhetaten—which had already been abandoned in Tutankhamen's reign—was razed to the ground. In the same way that Akhenaten himself had attempted to erase the names of the Egyptian gods, Horemheb ordered every trace of Akhenaten's god, his religion, his reign, his image, and his name erased from records and monuments throughout Egypt. The work was done thoroughly enough that only scattered references to "the accursed one of Akhetaten" remained to puzzle historians until the excavations at Amarna began to reveal what had happened. *SEE ALSO* EGYPTIAN OCCULTISM.

almadel: In the traditions of medieval goetic magic, a wax square inscribed with magical figures and names, supported by projections from the bases of four candles, and used in a specific set of evocations. The grimoire providing these instructions, the *Art Almadel*, was in circulation by the early thirteenth century, when William of Auvergne, Bishop of Paris, denounced it. The almadel is sometimes called "almandel" or "amandel" and has experienced a modest revival. *SEE ALSO* GRIMOIRE; LEMEGETON.

altar: A flat-topped item of ritual furniture, used in many different occult traditions as a support for ritual tools and other symbolic objects. Altars have been a nearly universal feature in Western (and Eastern) religious practice for thousands of years. In ancient times, the altar was primarily used as a place where sacrifices were offered to the gods.

Most modern Pagan and magical traditions place an altar at the center of the ritual circle. The altar in most ceremonial magic traditions is square-topped and twice as high as it is across the top; this duplicates the proportions of a double cube. The altar may be covered with a black cloth to symbolize the prima material or unformed first matter of the alchemists; a white cloth to represent purity; or a cloth of elemental, planetary, or sephirothic color, depending on the force to be invoked in any given working.

Ancient Mystical Order Rosae Crucis (AMORC): An internationally active Rosicrucian order, as of this writing AMORC is among the largest occult organizations in the world. Founded in the United States but currently based in France, AMORC offers correspondence courses to a nearly worldwide audience, and has lodges in most American states and a number of foreign countries.

AMORC traces its own history, and that of Rosicrucianism, back to the "heretic pharaoh" Akhenaten, and claims a direct succession from the historical Rosicrucians. *SEE* AKHENATEN; ROSICRUCIANS. H. Spencer Lewis, AMORC's founder, is said to have received authority from a variety of European Rosicrucian bodies. Historians outside the order, however, date its origins to 1915, when H. Spencer Lewis received a charter from Theodor Reuss, head of the Ordo Templi Orientis (OTO), and went to work trying to found a lodge. After several false starts, the new organization was incorporated in Florida in 1925.

Two years later Spencer and his family, who among themselves filled most of the offices of the fledgling order, moved operations to San Jose and acquired a printing plant and a radio transmitter.

Lewis and his order had a complicated relationship with its parent body, the Ordo Templi Orientis. The 1915 charter from Reuss was part of an intended collaboration between Lewis and the OTO, and was part of Reuss' efforts to regain control of the order from Aleister Crowley and his protegé Charles Stansfield Jones. *SEE* CROWLEY, ALEISTER. Crowley, for his part, made overtures to Lewis in 1918 and offered him membership in the OTO or the A∴A∴, but Lewis turned him down. Reuss granted Lewis the honorary degrees of 33°, 90°, 95°, and VII° in 1921, the same year he formally expelled Crowley from the OTO, but his constant requests for money alienated Lewis and led to a parting of the ways between them.

To his occult background, Lewis added marketing and advertising talents of a high order, and once AMORC was on its feet it attracted a growing stream of students. This brought the new order the unwanted attention of R. Swinburne Clymer, head of the Pennsylvania-based Fraternitas Rosae Crucis (FRC), who claimed exclusive rights to the term "Rosicrucian." For much of the 1930s the two orders fought a furious but inconclusive pamphlet war over their respective pedigrees, which ended up in the courts. During the midst of this, Aleister Crowley offered Lewis his support against Clymer. Lewis, sensibly, did not take the Beast up on his offer.

On Lewis' death in 1939, the position of Imperator passed to his son, Ralph Maxwell Lewis. Most of the original AMORC monographs and rituals were withdrawn from circulation shortly afterwards and have not been used since. Working with a new set of rituals and teachings, AMORC went on to become perhaps the most successful of all of the twentieth-century occult orders, with local chapters in most American cities and a substantial overseas presence as well.

On Ralph Maxwell Lewis' death in 1987, the position of Imperator passed to Gary L. Stewart. Three years later, in 1990, Stewart was removed by the AMORC board of directors on charges of embezzlement, amid a flurry of accusations, countercharges, and legal maneuvering. Stewart was replaced by Christian Bernard, the present Imperator. Despite these upheavals, AMORC remains an active presence today, and is probably the largest American occult order in existence as of this writing.

Arithmancy: Divination by means of numbers. This is the proper term for what is now usually called "numerology," that is, divination using the numerical value of a person's name, but it was once given much broader applications in occult theory and practice.

In Greek, Hebrew and several other ancient languages, every letter has a numerical value (Fans of jargon will be delighted to learn that languages with the pecularity are called *isopsephic languages*.) The habit of adding up the values of the letters of a word, and drawing conclusions about the word based on numerical connections with other words, was an obvious development in these languages, and it was heavily used by Jewish Cabalists, Greek and Hellenistic mystics, and early Christians; the famous enigma from the Book of Revelation, the "number of a man" 666, derives from this practice. The Cabala still uses arithmantic methods heavily.

The oldest known reference to arithmancy is found in an inscription of Sargon II, king of Assyria from 727 to 707 BC.. According to the inscription, the city wall of the new Assyrian capitol, Dur Sharrukin, was made to measure 16,283 cubits long, since this number was the value of Sargon's name. The origins of the system are thus probably to be found in Mesopotamian occult tradition.

Attempts have been made since ancient times to work out methods of arithmancy for languages that are not isopsephic. In Latin, where only certain letters (*I, V, X, L, C* and so on) have numerical values, medieval and Renaissance writers took up the habit of counting up the number values of these particular letters when they occurred in a word or phrase. For example, IVDICIVM, "judgment" in Latin, can be added up to 1613—a detail that gave a certain amount of impetus to sixteenth-century speculation about the approaching Last Judgment and may have played a role in setting off the Rosicrucian furor. SEE ROSICRUCIANS.

In modern languages such as English, many different systems of arithmancy have been produced, none of them entirely satisfactory. The most basic, which is much used in popular numerology but also can be found in Renaissance occult writings, simply gives each letter the number of its place in the alphabet; thus *A*, the first letter, is 1, and *Z*, the twenty-sixth, is 26. A variation on this adds together the digits of any two-digit number; thus *Z* in this system would equal 8 (26 becomes $2 + 6 = 8$). Other systems, based on analogies between English sounds and those of Hebrew, Greek and other languages, are also in circulation.

arithmology: The esoteric science of number, sometimes confused with arithmancy or "numerology." Arithmology is the application of occult principles to number (or vice versa), so that numerical relationships become symbols of magical and spiritual forces. Arithmology is to number what sacred geometry is to geometrical form, and both are part of the quadrivium, the four sciences of occult mathematics. *SEE* QUADRIVIUM; SACRED GEOMETRY.

The differences between arithmology and arithmancy are easy to trace out in the abstract, but often become complicated in practice. In arithmancy, numbers are used to translate letters—for example, a Hebrew or Greek word may be converted to its numerical equivalent, and then compared to other words with the same numerical value. In arithmology, on the other hand, the numerical properties of the number itself are the key to its meaning; thus two, for example, is associated with ideas of division and polarity, while three represents the resolution of polarity by a third connecting factor. While these differences are fairly straightforward, it has been common since ancient times to use arithmological ideas to decipher arithmantic relationships, to construct arithmantic word-conundrums to conceal arithmological secrets, and to mix the two together in any number of other ingenious ways.

The origins of the Western tradition of arithmology are not known for certain, although both Egypt and Mesopotamia had advanced mathematical knowledge closely interwoven with spiritual teachings early enough to be responsible. The Greek philosopher and mystic Pythagoras of Samos (c. 570–c. 495 BCE), who traveled and studied in both these countries, is the first clearly known figure in the tradition. His students, who scattered across the Mediterranean world after the anti-Pythagorean riots of the early fifth century BCE, passed on elements of his teachings to others. *SEE* PYTHAGORAS.

The Neoplatonists of the early centuries of the Common Era played a major role in reviving arithmological studies; from them, the tradition passed down to the Middle Ages, which included arithmology in ordinary arithmetic in the same way that it fused astrology and astronomy. The Renaissance occult revival drew heavily on ancient arithmological works and on medieval developments of the tradition, and Renaissance texts of arithmology—most of which have never been translated or even reprinted since the Scientific Revolution—represent in many ways the high-water mark of the tradition. The Scientific Revolution, here as elsewhere in the occult tradition, brought an end to this flourishing of arithmological studies. Still, a slow but steady trickle of books on the subject has continued to appear up to the present time.

By way of Freemasonry, which absorbed certain elements of traditional arithmology at an early date, arithmological symbolism still plays an important role in many fraternal and magical lodge systems. The number of officers in a lodge, degrees or grades in a system, knocks upon a door, rungs on a symbolic ladder, or stripes upon a robe in a traditional lodge generally has a specific arithmological

meaning. *SEE* LODGE, MAGICAL. *SEE ALSO* QUADRIV-
IUM; SACRED GEOMETRY.

Ars Notoria: *SEE* NOTORY ART.

Art of Memory: Originally developed in ancient Greece,
the Art of Memory is a system for expanding the capac-
ity and accuracy of human memory by the use of visu-
alization. Its connections to the occult traditions of the
West were somewhat limited until the Renaissance, and
in classical and medieval times it was an ordinary part of
most educated people's knowledge set, with no connection at all to occultism. During the Renaissance, however,
a number of major occult figures practiced it extensively,
and Giordano Bruno and Robert Fludd both contributed
important works on the subject. *SEE* FLUDD, ROBERT.

   A practitioner of the Art of Memory in its classical
form starts by memorizing the inside of a building, walk-
ing through it physically and then, repeatedly, in imagination until he or she can recall it in detail. A set of *loci*
("places") within the building are chosen so that when the
practitioner walks through the building in imagination,
he or she will pass by each locus. Each "place" is then
stocked with a visualized image representing something
the practitioner wants to remember. The image should be
striking and memorable, and it should suggest the thing

to be memorized in some unmistakable way; visual puns and the use of "alphabets" of images were a standard way of doing this. Once the images are in place, the practitioner simply has to walk through the building once again in imagination and take note of the images to remember what they are intended to convey.

All this seems extremely complicated and roundabout to modern minds, but it works extremely well in practice. Modern practitioners have found that with practice, an enormous amount of information can be quickly and accurately stored and recalled by these methods. During its Renaissance interaction with the Western occult traditions, the Art of Memory left several important traces behind. Mnemonic habits of constructing striking visual images had a major impact on occult symbolism, and the tarot cards themselves may have started out life as images in someone's private memory system. By way of Giordano Bruno's student Alexander Dicson, the Art of Memory also came into use in stonemasons' craft lodges in Scotland, and thus may have had an important role in shaping the symbolism and ritual of Freemasonry; *SEE* FREEMASONRY.

ascendant: In astrology, the point on the ecliptic on the eastern horizon at any specific point in time. In natal astrology, the ascendant plays a crucial role, as it marks the orientation of the subject to the entire pattern of fixed

stars and zodiacal constellations. In ancient and early medieval astrology, the ascendant was termed the horoscope;
the importance of this point may be judged by the fact
that, by the late Middle Ages, it had given its name to the
entire chart. *SEE* ASTROLOGY.

astral plane: In occult philosophy, the realm of con-
crete consciousness, the level of reality that corresponds
to the human experiences of dream, vision, out-of-body
experience, and ordinary consciousness. The astral plane
is located between the etheric plane, the level of subtle
life-energy, and the mental plane, the level of abstract
consciousness and meaning. As with all the planes of occult theory, the astral is "above" or "below" other planes
only in a metaphorical sense; in reality, all the planes in-
terpenetrate the realm of physical matter experienced by
the senses.

The astral plane is the most important of the planes
from the point of view of the practicing magician, since
it is on the astral level that most magical energies come
into manifestation. It stands on the border between the
timeless and spaceless mental and spiritual planes, on the
one hand, and the etheric and physical planes within space
and time, on the other. It is on the astral level, therefore,
that patterns from the higher planes take shape before de-
scending fully into space and time, and the magician who

can access this plane freely and effectively can influence the way these patterns work out in the world of ordinary experience.

astrology: The art and science of divination by the position of sun, moon, planets, and stars relative to a position on the surface of the Earth, astrology is among the most ancient branches of occultism still being practiced today. Its essential concept is that the position of stars and planets at any given moment can be interpreted as a map of the subtle forces and factors in play at that moment. When a person is born, an event takes place, or a question is asked, the characteristics of the exact moment in time when these things happen are mirrored in the heavens, and can be read by those who know how.

Central to traditional Western astrology is a vision of the universe as a matrix of forces in which everything affects everything else. The same energies that flow through stars and planets also pulse through the minds and bodies of individual human beings, and the movements of the heavens are thus mirrored in subtle ways by events on Earth. Many older accounts of astrology approach this awareness by way of the Neoplatonist philosophy that underlies most Western occultism, while many modern astrologers prefer to speak in terms of psychologist Carl

Jung's concept of "synchronicity"; either way, the basic concept is the same.

The origins of astrology can be found in the ancient city-states of Mesopotamia, where Pagan religious beliefs held that the planets were gods and goddesses, and where priests began tracking the movements of the deities in heaven at a very early date. The oldest surviving record of planetary movements, the Venus tablet of Ammishaduqa, dates from approximately 1650 BCE, but there is every reason to think such records once reached many centuries further back. The recorded movements of the planets, along with many other omens and signs, were compared with earthly events and the results recorded. By the seventh century BCE, when the 7,000-omen collection Enuma Anu Enlil was compiled, this huge project had reached the stage where systematic conclusions could be drawn, and it was in the centuries immediately following that astrology as we know it first took shape.

The oldest known horoscopes, as suggested above, are Babylonian, and date from the end of the fifth century BCE. Shortly thereafter, the art was transmitted to the rising new power of Greece, and when Alexander the Great conquered Mesopotamia in 331 BCE the resulting political and cultural shifts spread astrology throughout the Mediterranean world.

It was one among many systems of divination until the reign of Augustus, the first emperor of Rome (63 BCE–19 CE). Augustus found astrology useful as a propaganda tool in his quest to legitimatize his rule over the former republic, and published his horoscope to back up his claim that the stars destined him to rule Rome. His patronage and that of his successor Tiberius made astrology the most prestigious of divination systems, and sparked a golden age of astrological practice and study.

Many important textbooks of astrology were written in the following two centuries, including the books of Manilius, Dorotheus of Sidon, Vettius Valens, and above all Claudius Ptolemy, whose *Tetrabiblos* (*Four Books*) was the most important manual of astrology for more than a thousand years thereafter. Passed on to the Arabs during the declining years of Rome, astrology underwent further refinements as generations of Arab astronomers and mathematicians worked out new tools for calculating the exact positions of planets and signs and for extracting meaning from the chart.

Astrology underwent a partial eclipse in Europe during the early Middle Ages, largely as a result of Christian prejudices against divination. The basic elements of the art were preserved, however, and contemporary records indicate that most of the French nobility as early as the ninth century CE sought advice from private astrologers.

Most of early medieval astrology had to depend on night-by-night observations of the stars and planets, since much of the mathematical knowledge needed to erect a horoscope accurately was lost with the fall of Rome, and had to be reimported from the Arabic world. Early medieval astrologers paid a great deal of attention to the phases and positions of the moon, which could be easily tracked by eye, and an entire literature of lunar astrological almanacs came into being.

By the end of the eleventh century CE, however, Arabic astrological and mathematical books were being translated into Latin, and soon became available to scholars throughout Europe. While many church officials were suspicious of the astrological revival, many others were enthusiastic supporters of the new art, and astrology became extremely popular.

By the early part of the twelfth century, detailed astrological tables became available in Western Europe and removed the last serious barrier in the way of astrological practice. With the new Alphonsine Tables—so called because they were compiled under the direction of King Alfonso I of Aragon—anyone with a basic knowledge of Latin and mathematics could erect a horoscope accurate to within a degree or so. From this point on, astrology was, for all practical purposes, an everyday part of life until the coming of the Scientific Revolution. A small number of scholars denounced it or challenged its assumptions, but most people treated it as part of the basic nature of reality. It's typical of the age that during the middle of the sixteenth century, when the Reformation was heating up, Protestant and Catholic astrologers worked up and circulated sharply different horoscopes of Martin Luther, respectively praising or damning him by means of the stars.

The sixteenth century also saw the beginning of a movement to put astrological knowledge into the hands of the public. Jerome Cardan (1501–1576), an Italian astrologer and scholar, was instrumental in starting this process with his book *Libelli Duos* (*Two Booklets*, 1538), which contained the first widely circulated collection of horoscopes and their interpretations in print. The greatly expanded 1547 edition of the *Libelli* also included a set of aphorisms meant to serve as a detailed guide to chart interpretation. Later figures expanded this project by translating astrological texts out of Latin into the languages of the common people. William Lilly (1602–1681) was the most important of these in the English-speaking world, publishing the first English textbook of astrology, *Christian Astrology* (1647; the title was an attempt to counter claims that astrology was a Satanic art). At the same time, however, the first stirrings of the Scientific Revolution were underway, and with it a complete rejection of astrology and the rest of the Western occult tradition.

The scientific rejection of astrology primarily affected the educated upper classes, however, and astrologers continued their practice lower down the social ladder. All through the so-called Age of Reason, a succession of popular almanacs in most Western countries carried on the traditions of astrology, and works such as Lilly's were much in demand in the underworld of folk magicians, occult secret societies, and magical lodges.

With the beginning of the occult revival of the late nineteenth century, astrology was among the first occult sciences to begin the climb back into wider publicity. The work of English astrologer Alan Leo was central in launching this astrological renaissance. That climb accelerated in the twentieth century, which saw the emergence of professional organizations such as the American Federation of Astrologers, the development of a sizeable industry in astrological books and magazines, and—especially in the wake of the Sixties—the return of astrology to social acceptability in many circles. The revelation that American president Ronald Reagan planned many of the events of his presidency according to the advice of a California astrologer made headlines, but significantly it seems to have had little impact on his popularity—even with conservative Christian supporters who might have been expected to protest. The place of astrology in the Western world thus seems secure for the time being.

The essential medium of the astrologer's art is the astrological chart, which provides an abstract map of the heavens for a given moment from the standpoint of a particular place on the Earth's surface. The chart includes the following features:

a) twelve houses, which are abstract divisions of the sky as seen from Earth, each representing some aspect of human life. The modern system of twelve houses is partly descended from an older system of eight houses, the octatopos, used in Greek and Roman times. There are various ways of dividing the heavens mathematically into twelve sections, but in all but a few exotic systems the first house begins at the ascendant—the point rising above the eastern horizon at the moment for which the horoscope is drawn up—and the houses proceed counterclockwise around the chart.

b) four *cardines* or cardinal points—the ascendant, zenith or midheaven, descendent, and nadir—which represent the eastern horizon, the middle of the sky overhead, the western horizon, and the point in the sky directly beneath the Earth.

c) twelve signs of the zodiac, which are divisions of the heavens marked out by twelve constellations close to the ecliptic, the track of the sun among the stars. Due to the rotation of the Earth, the entire zodiac passes over each spot on the Earth's surface in a little less than twenty-four hours. The relation between the signs and the houses provide the basic framework of the horoscope.

d) seven or more planets, which move against the background of the zodiac in patterns determined by their orbits and the orbit and rotation of the Earth. In astrological terms, the sun and the moon are planets, and at least five others—Mercury, Venus, Mars, Jupiter, and Saturn, the five planets visible from Earth without a telescope—also play an important role in all forms of Western astrology. Many astrologers include the more recently discovered planets Uranus, Neptune, and Pluto in the astrological chart, some include the larger asteroids, and a few keep track of other, hypothetical bodies such as Lilith, an invisible moon said to be orbiting the Earth, and Transpluto, a planet out beyond the orbit of Pluto.

e) an assortment of other points, including the north and south nodes of the moon, which represent the points where the moon's and sun's tracks through the zodiac intersect; the Arabian parts, mathematically calculated points that are of high importance in Arabic astrology; and others.

f) aspects—geometrical angles—between any two planets, parts, lunar nodes, or cardines, which determine the relationship between the different energies active in the chart.

While most people think of astrology primarily as a way of determining character and destiny by reading a person's birth chart, there are many different applications of the art. The most important branches of astrological practice are as follows:

Electional astrology is astrology in reverse; instead of erecting a chart for a particular time and interpreting its meaning, the electional astrologer tries to find a particular time when the astrological influences will most strongly favor some particular action. This system is among the most important in occult practice, as many systems of magic require the time of ritual workings to be selected astrologically. *SEE* ELECTIONAL ASTROLOGY.

Genethliac astrology is an older term for natal astrology (see below).

Horary astrology is a strictly divinatory use of the art. A chart is erected for the moment when a particular question is asked, and various rules are used to work out a favorable or unfavorable answer to the question. *SEE* HORARY ASTROLOGY.

Mundane astrology is the astrology of nations and the world as a whole, and uses special tools such as eclipses and conjunctions of Jupiter and Saturn to trace out grand cycles of time.

Natal astrology is the most famous form of the art, where an astrological chart is drawn up for the moment and place of a person's birth to divine details of their character and destiny in life. The oldest surviving horoscopes are natal horoscopes, a fact that testifies to the enduring interest of this branch of astrology.

Boaz: (Hebrew, "in it is strength") One of the two pillars at the door of the Temple of Solomon, an important element of Cabalistic, magical, and Masonic symbolism. The pillar Boaz stood at the left of the entrance of the temple. In symbolism, it is often shown as black, and corresponds to the receptive or passive, the material, and the feminine, as the pillar Jachin corresponds to the active, the spiritual, and the masculine. Cabalists associate Boaz with the left-hand pillar of the Tree of Life, the Pillar of Severity. *SEE TREE OF LIFE.*

In many Masonic lodges, the pillar Boaz is topped with a globe of the earth, representing its association with the material world.

Cabala: (Hebrew, "oral tradition") One of the core elements of Western occultism, the Cabala began as a mystical movement in Jewish communities in Spain and southern France. Adopted first by Christian mystics, then by Hermetic magicians, and finally by almost every branch of Western occultism, it became the dominant occult philosophy in the West for several centuries, while remaining a central part of Jewish mystical belief and practice. Jewish, Christian, Hermetic, and Pagan versions of Cabala are still very much in use today.

The word "Cabala" is a Latin transliteration of the Hebrew word QBLH, "tradition," in the sense of unwritten tradition. Other transliterations include Kabbalah, Qabalah, and Kabala. In recent years, some writers have attempted to draw distinctions among these terms, using "Kabbalah" for the original Jewish version of the tradition, "Cabala" for the Christian version, and "Qabalah" for the Hermetic version. Others have ignored these attempts at classification, and the boundaries between the different aspects of Cabala have rarely been firm enough to justify hard and fast divisions. "Cabala," the oldest and most common spelling of the word, will be used here for all branches of the tradition.

The origins of the Cabala are variously given in the old sources. Some texts claim that the original Cabala was transmitted to Adam, either by God or by the angel Raziel, at the beginning of time. Adam's son Seth is another candidate for the founder of the Cabalistic tradition. Nearly all sources record the claim that Moses, while on Mount Sinai, received from God two different sets of teachings— the written law, enshrined in the first five books of the Old Testament, and a secret oral law, passed on by word of mouth, which included the hidden meanings and interpretations of the written law. From that time, the legends claim, the Cabala was passed down continuously from master to pupil until the present.

Turning from these mythic perspectives to those of history, the first versions of Cabala actually emerged in Jewish mystical groups in Provence, in the south of France, during the eleventh century CE. These groups drew heavily on older Jewish mystical traditions such as the Ma'aseh Merkabah and the Ma'aseh Berashith, and were also deeply familiar with the Neoplatonist tradition. At some point around 1150, they also obtained a fragmentary book or collection of books that, via a process of editing, became the first major text of Cabalistic theory, the Bahir.

Isaac the Blind, a rabbi of Narbonne who died around 1235, was the crucial figure in the formulation of this early Cabala. He had disciples throughout Spain and southern France, who passed on his teachings. Centers of Cabalistic study founded by his pupils sprang up in Gerona, Burgos, and Toledo in Spain.

What set these teachings apart from other, earlier versions of Jewish mysticism was a new set of doctrines about the nature of God and the world, and a new approach to religious practice. To the Cabalist, God in himself is utterly hidden behind the three veils of Ain (Nothing), Ain Soph (Infinity), and Ain Soph Aur (Limitless Light). In manifestation, God expresses himself through the Sephiroth, ten creative powers that came forth from the divine unity and formed the Tree of Life. SEE SEPHIROTH, TREE OF LIFE. The Sephiroth are connected by twenty-two Paths, which correspond to the twenty-two letters of the Hebrew alphabet. The Tree of Life also maps out the stages of ascent in the spiritual path, which can unfold over many lives; unlike other Jews, Cabalists accept reincarnation, although there have been far-reaching disputes about how reincarnation works and how it relates to more orthodox ideas of heaven and hell.

Cabalists do not differ from other Jews in their religious practices or their daily life—in fact, from the beginning, the Cabala tended to be a conservative force within Judaism, favoring strict obedience to tradition and custom. The difference in practice lies in the way that Cabalists use traditional religious duties as a vehicle for meditative practice and mystical experience. In Cabalistic practice, every one of the rituals and customs surrounding Jewish life has a mystical meaning, and should be done with that meaning in mind. In reciting prayers or reading from the scriptures, each word of the Hebrew text is used as a focus for concentrated attention and devotional meditation.

The Cabalistic tradition went through an important series of developments in Spain, where it became popular in large parts of the Jewish community and won the support of many of the best rabbinic scholars and legalists of the thirteenth and fourteenth centuries. During this time, many of the details of later Cabalistic teachings were worked out, and in particular the order and relationships of the Sephiroth took on a standard form, the Cabalistic Tree of Life; *SEE* TREE OF LIFE. The eccentric but brilliant mystic Abraham Abulafia was initiated into this Spanish tradition of Cabala, and many of his handbooks of meditation became standard after his death in Spanish Cabalistic circles and elsewhere. Two main currents emerged; the school of Gerona, which focused on a more philosophical approach, and the school of Burgos, which had a more ecstatic and magical bent.

These currents were fused in the greatest text of Spanish Cabala, the Zohar. Attributed to the third-century mystic Simeon bar Yochai, it was actually the creation of Moses de Leon, a Spanish Cabalist who spent most of his life in the small town of Guadalajara, north of Madrid. A huge, complex, many-layered book written over a period of some thirty years, the Zohar presents the Cabala in a deeply mythic vein. It quickly became the standard text of Cabalistic study, and brought Cabalistic ideas to Jewish communities all over the Mediterranean basin and beyond. *SEE* ZOHAR.

Spain continued to be the center of Cabalistic study and development until 1492, when the Spanish government ordered all Jews expelled from the country. It was also in Spain, in the years before the expulsion, that the first stirrings of Christian Cabala emerged. The earliest movements in this direction were on the part of Christian missionaries, who sought to learn enough about Judaism to make efforts to convert Jews to Christianity more successful. In the Cabala, they found not only a potential tool for proselytizing, but a new way to look at their own religious tradition. The "combinatorial art" of Ramon Lull (1235–1315), which later played a significant role in Renaissance occult philosophies, was inspired at least partly by Cabalistic teachings about the Hebrew alphabet and its combinations.

The expulsion was a tremendous shock to the Jewish community throughout Europe, and it turned Cabalistic thought into more prophetic and messianic directions. Cabalistic works predicting the coming of the Messiah and the redemption of Israel began to circulate in the decades after 1492. By scattering Spanish Cabalists across much of Europe, the expulsion also gave a major boost to the Christian Cabala.

Before the expulsion, in 1486, the Italian philosopher Giovanni Pico della Mirandola (1463–1494) had begun studying Cabalistic texts with the Jewish Christian convert Samuel ben Nissim Abulfaraj (also known as Flavius Mithridates), and launched a furor that echoed across Europe by proclaiming that "no science can better convince us of the divinity of Jesus Christ than magic and the Cabala." In the year of Pico's death, the German scholar Johannes Reuchlin (1455–1522) published his *De Verbo Mirifico* (*On the Wonder-Working Word*), an introduction to Christian Cabala, which focused on the Cabalistic interpretation of the name of Jesus. Reuchlin followed this up in 1517 with the far more comprehensive *De Arte Cabalistica* (*On the Art of the Cabala*), which has been called the first serious Cabalistic treatise in any Western language.

After Reuchlin, the Christian Cabala was the subject of a flood of publications, and the first traces of a purely Hermetic, magical Cabala appeared in 1533 with the publication of Cornelius Agrippa's *Three Books of Occult Philosophy*. For several centuries thereafter, this magical Cabala remained at least nominally Christian, just as most versions of Hermeticism from the Renaissance until the beginning of the twentieth century had some degree of Christian gloss; *SEE* HERMETICISM.

After the expulsion of the Jews from Spain, the center of Jewish Cabalistic studies shifted eastward, and the town of Safed in Israel became the site of the most important Cabalistic schools from 1530 onward. Other centers came into existence in Italy, North Africa, and Turkey, where large numbers of exiled Spanish Jews settled.

The most important Cabalist of the Safed school was Rabbi Isaac Luria (1534–1572), a brilliant and charismatic mystic who radically reshaped the Cabala. Many of the basic concepts of later Cabalistic thought were first introduced by Luria: *tzimtzum*, the "contraction" of the divine at the very beginning of the process of Creation; the primal worlds of unbalanced force, which were destroyed, giving rise to the Qlippoth, the "husks" or "shells" that are the demons of Lurianic Cabala; the five *partzufim*, or personifications in the Tree of Life; and the process of *tikkunor*, redemption, in which all the sparks of light lost amid the world of the Qlippoth are to be restored to the world of light. Luria also introduced new meditative techniques to Cabala, foremost among them the practice of *Yichud*, or Unification, a system of meditation on divine names.

The teachings of Isaac Luria became widespread throughout the Jewish world within a generation of his early death. They combined with the intense messianic expectations of the time in the career of Shabbatai Zevi (1626–1676). Zevi was proclaimed as the Messiah in 1665 by the noted Cabalist Nathan of Gaza, and hundreds of thousands of Jews throughout Europe and the Middle East accepted the claim and prepared for the messianic kingdom. The sordid end of the whole affair—seized by the Turkish government in 1666, Zevi was offered a choice between execution and conversion and renounced Judaism on the spot—did much to diminish the messianic expectations of the time, but little to weaken the place of Cabala in Jewish thought and religious practice. A hard core of Zevi's followers continued to believe in their Messiah, arguing that his apostasy was somehow part of his messianic mission, and many of these converted to Islam or Christianity over the next century or so, bringing with them a set of radical Cabalistic teachings associated with the Shabbatean movement.

For some three hundred years, from the middle of the sixteenth to the middle of the nineteenth century, Cabalistic approaches were at the core of Judaism as it was practiced throughout Europe and the Middle East. During this period, a more popular version of Cabala became common in eastern European Judaism, fostered by the Hasidic movement founded by Rabbi Israel Ba'al Shem Tov (1698–1760). Only with the eighteenth century and the rise of the Haskalah ("Enlightenment") movement among Jews in western Europe did the Cabala begin to lose its importance in Jewish circles. To this day there are still many Hasidic and Cabalistic schools in Jewish communities throughout the world, preserving the traditions of Jewish Cabala and communicating them to new generations of students.

The history of Christian and Hermetic Cabala in recent centuries has been more complex. While orthodox Christian denominations rid themselves of Cabalistic elements by 1650, the Cabala kept the dominant role it held in the Renaissance all through the later development of Western occultism, and both Christian mysticism and Hermetic magic remained closely linked with Cabala. The writings of Jacob Böhme (1575–1624), the mystical shoemaker of Görlitz, do not seem to have been directly influenced by Cabalistic writings, but the alchemical Christian theosophy Böhme taught could easily be combined with Cabalistic ideas. Alchemy, astrology, magic, and many other branches of the occult traditions of the West flowed into the Cabalistic tradition toward the end of the Renaissance, and inspired the great Hermetic encyclopedias of Robert Fludd; *SEE* FLUDD, ROBERT. This same fusion of traditions continued at the core of the Western occult movement thereafter.

The Hermetic tradition of the Cabala was recognized by Eliphas Lévi (1810–1875), the founder of the modern occult renaissance, as the core of the tradition he hoped to revive. It was Lévi who first connected the letters of the Hebrew alphabet with the twenty-two Major Arcana of the tarot, setting in motion a major new direction in Cabalistic symbolism.

After Lévi, a series of occultists in France and England, most of them associated with the major occult orders of the late nineteenth and early twentieth century, developed new variations on the old Cabalistic themes, or veered off in new directions entirely. Very few traditional Cabalistic sources were known to these Hermetic Cabalists, few of whom were literate in Hebrew. On the other hand, Latin translations made during the Renaissance and early modern periods were much used, and the ancient Sepher Yetzirah was also closely studied. A good deal of the material in the new Hermetic Cabala, however, came from Renaissance magical writings with little relationship to the Cabala, and another major source was the field of comparative religion and mythology, which led Hermetic

Cabalists to propose directions—such as the attribution of Pagan gods and goddesses to the Tree of Life—that were unthinkable in classic Jewish Cabala.

The work of the Hermetic Order of the Golden Dawn, the most significant of these orders, was largely based on this new Hermetic Cabala, and the publication of most of the Golden Dawn legacy over the course of the twentieth century led its particular take on Cabalistic matters to become all but universal in the magical community throughout the English-speaking world. The French magical tradition of Lévi and Papus also became popular in many parts of the Western world.

These developments led, for the first time, to versions of the Cabala that had no connection whatsoever to either Judaism or Christianity—first in the Hermetic tradition, with the works of such figures as Aleister Crowley (1875–1947) and Manly Palmer Hall (1901–1990), and then in the last decades of the twentieth century with the first Neopagan versions of the Cabala; *SEE* CROWLEY, ALEISTER. Many of these were based on the work of the Hermetic Order of the Golden Dawn and its offshoots, and adapted this material to a dizzying assortment of new spiritual and symbolic approaches.

ceremonial magic: One of the major divisions of Western magic, also known as ritual magic. As the name implies, ceremonial magic uses ritual or ceremonial means as its primary approach to working with magical energies and entities. The main traditions of ceremonial magic in the Western world have long been deeply intertwined with the Hermetic tradition on the one hand, and the Cabala on the other, and the term "ceremonial magic" is often used as a label for these traditions in modern occult parlance. *SEE* CABALA; HERMETICISM.

The concept of ceremonial magic, as distinct from other kinds of magical practice, emerged in the Middle Ages and was heavily influenced by the legal strictures on magical practice imposed by the Catholic Church. The church's main concern was to prohibit the worship of Pagan deities, and any form of magic that could be construed as a mode of worship was strictly prohibited unless it dealt strictly with the Christian Trinity or the saints. Thus all magic that dealt with spirits of any kind was forbidden, while approaches such as natural magic and religious magic were generally permitted. *SEE* CHRISTIAN OCCULTISM; NATURAL MAGIC.

The prohibited forms of magic formed the first nucleus of what developed into the ceremonial magic of the later Middle Ages and Renaissance. Heavily supplemented by material from Arabic magical manuals such as the *Picatrix*, ceremonial magic developed a literature of its own, consisting of the famous *grimoires* or "grammars" of magical practice. *SEE* GRIMOIRE. Some of these were openly demonological works of goetic magic that aimed at summoning the powers of evil and exploiting them for the magician's benefit. Others dealt with planetary spirits and other ethically neutral powers, and still others were works of angel magic of a more or less austere character. The church predictably classified them all as demonic, and until the Renaissance the whole tradition was relatively secret.

During the Renaissance occult revival, attitudes toward the old ceremonial magic of the grimoires varied widely. Some of the important Renaissance magi rejected the medieval tradition completely, turning instead to Hermetic and Cabalistic sources in an attempt to produce a new, theologically untainted magic. Others borrowed freely from the grimoires. In this latter camp was Cornelius Agrippa, whose *De Occulta Philosophia Libri Tres* (*Three Books of Occult Philosophy*, 1533) was among the central texts of magicians for several centuries thereafter. The ceremonial magic of the modern occult revival drew heavily on these medieval and Renaissance sources, but was profoundly reshaped by the writings of Eliphas Lévi (1810–1875). Lévi's works argued for a higher, spiritual dimension to magical practice, seeing the goal of magic as the spiritual transformation of the magus, rather than simply as the accomplishment of practical goals. This approach became extremely common after his death, partly through the influence of the Hermetic Order of the Golden Dawn and its many offshoots, and partly as the increasing Western knowledge of Eastern traditions such as yoga influenced the way Western occultists thought about their own traditions.

The rise of the Neopagan movement in the second half of the twentieth century brought about another change, one that is still reshaping the ceremonial magic tradition. The efforts of Pagans to define their religions as something different from other occult traditions led, particularly in the English-speaking countries, to a division of the magical community into Pagan and "ceremonialist" wings, with this latter term meaning "practitioner of ceremonial magic." From the Renaissance to the 1950s, Pagan religious practice of one form or another was a common element of many currents of ceremonial magic, but this has become increasingly uncommon in recent years as Neopagan writers and practitioners have staked out their own claims to the territory.

At present, in the English-speaking world, the system of ceremonial magic created by the Hermetic Order of the Golden Dawn is the most popular, although several others are widely practiced. Recent decades have seen a great deal of research and exploration by ceremonial magicians, especially into the older byways of ritual magic and similar traditions from other cultures, and new developments in the field seem likely. *SEE ALSO* MAGIC; NATURAL MAGIC.

Christian occultism: Despite two thousand years worth of stereotypes, Christianity and the occult are far from strangers to each other, and there have been many different traditions of magic, divination, and occult practice founded on Christian principles. The existence of Christian occultism is one of the major blind spots in both contemporary Christian thinking and that of the occult community.

The occult dimensions of Christianity, in all probability, go all the way back to its founder. Rumors that Jesus of Nazareth was a magical practitioner, rather than a prophet, religious reformer, or deity, were apparently in circulation within a short time of his crucifixion, and several modern studies have shown that there is good reason to think that these rumors had a basis in fact.

Certainly practices that would normally be called magic and divination were in use in the earliest years of the Christian Church, among people who had known Jesus or his personal followers. Acts 1:23–26 documents the use of divination by lots to select a new apostle to replace Judas Iscariot, while Paul of Tarsus in 1 Corinthians 12:8–10 enumerates a set of gifts of the Holy Spirit that includes healing powers, the ability to prophesy, and the power to work miracles. While modern Christian theology draws a sharp distinction between these activities and occult practices, there is no real basis for that distinction; *SEE* MAGIC. There is also some evidence that geometrical and numerical symbolism can be found in numerous passages of the New Testament, suggesting that Pythagorean and Platonic mysticism was present in Christian circles from a very early period. *SEE* QUADRIVIUM; PLATONISM.

During the first few centuries of its existence, the Christian Church held attitudes toward magic that were fairly close to those of Roman society as a whole. The Roman state viewed all magical practices with suspicion, and prosecutions of people who practiced magic, divination, or related arts were a relatively common event in Roman times. At the same time, certain kinds of magical practice were considered acceptable: medical magic, weather magic, and most kinds of natural magic were exempt from Roman prohibitions, and most of the other types of magic were permitted unofficially so long as the magicians did not stray too close to the realm of politics. These same divisions, reshaped into church policy, became standard through most of the early Middle Ages.

With the collapse of Roman power in the West, the Christian Church found itself practically the sole custodian of classical learning in most of Europe. During the difficult years from the Visigothic sacking of Rome in 410 CE to the Carolingian revival of learning in the early ninth century, Christian monks, nuns, and church officials carried out what amounted to a vast salvage operation on what remained of Greek and Roman culture, and among the things that were preserved were magical documents and traditions.

A simple but straightforward rule seems to have governed the incorporation of magic into the new culture of Christian Europe: any magical working that avoided references to non Christian spirits or deities was acceptable; any working that invoked a non-Christian spirit or deity was either eliminated or reformulated in a Christian mode. This was made much easier by the large-scale transformation of Pagan gods into Christian saints, which allowed prayers to Apollo and Woden to be turned without much difficulty to Saint Apollinaris and Saint Swithold. Many magical and divinatory practices were Christianized in this way but otherwise left entirely intact. For example, the Lots of Astrampsychus, a popular divination system in late Roman times, was lightly revised by replacing its lists of oracular gods with equivalent lists of Christian saints, and remained equally popular in the early Middle Ages.

The result was the emergence of an extensive tradition of Christian magic in medieval Western cultures, entirely acceptable to the church and practiced by all levels of society throughout the medieval world. That tradition included astrology and other forms of divination, weather magic, agricultural magic, healing magic, and a wide range of assorted charms for luck, protection, and success. Even goetic magic, which involved summoning spirits and thus fell under the prohibition of the Christian church, took on a strong Christian coloration during the Middle Ages; many surviving goetic rituals include Christian holy names and symbols, and operate entirely within the mental universe of medieval Christianity.

This Christian magical tradition remained an important and largely public current in Western cultures until the fourteenth century. Thereafter, attitudes against magic hardened. The first signs of what was to come were a series of heresy trials in which the main evidence for heresy was the practice of magic. The prosecution of Dame Alice Kyteler in 1324–5 and the burning of the Italian astrologer Cecco d'Ascoli in 1327 marked the opening of a large-scale assault on magic. During the four centuries that followed, the assault grew in scope and severity until some fifty thousand people had been killed. Pagan historians have termed this period "the Burning Times."

Under these conditions Christian occultism faced a brutal struggle for survival. In the handbooks produced and used by inquisitors and witch-hunters, any ritual activity outside of those specifically sanctioned by the church was demon worship; the fact that many accused sorcerers and witches worked magic in the name of Christ and the saints was irrelevant. Still, nearly all occultists of the time continued to claim that they and their art were entirely Christian.

Some occult writers during the Burning Times included harsh condemnations of witchcraft in their works, as a way of drawing distinctions between what they were teaching and the ideas of magic in general circulation at the time. Others criticized the witch-hunting mania, and Cornelius Agrippa—author of the most important Renaissance handbook of ceremonial magic—is known to have successfully defended an accused witch in court.

The impact of the Burning Times on Christian occult traditions was profound. Of the rich traditions of Christian magic and divination before the fourteenth century, very little survived. The exceptions were at opposite ends of the social scale. On the one hand, the vast majority of ceremonial magicians—who came from the educated upper classes—continued to think of themselves as Christian magicians, and to use Christian holy names and symbols in their workings. Ceremonial occult traditions such as Martinism and the Rosicrucian movement, in particular, drew heavily on Christian theology and practice. *SEE* ROSICRUCIANS. Among the poor, especially in isolated areas, folk magic with Christian elements continued to be practiced quietly.

Both of these currents faded out to a large extent with the coming of industrialization in the nineteenth century, and the rise of alternatives to Christianity in the late nineteenth and twentieth centuries took care of much of what remained. While the Hermetic Order of the Golden Dawn, founded in 1888, originally required its members either to be Christian or to "be prepared to take an interest in Christian symbolism," many of its twentieth-century successor orders have been non-Christian or even anti-Christian.

Similarly, the penetration of Theosophy, Asian religions, and Neopaganism into popular culture throughout the Western world in the twentieth century has had a strong impact on folk traditions of magic. It's not hard to find people in America who come from families with more or less Christian traditions of folk magic but who encountered the Neopagan movement, decided that this was what their family traditions were actually about, and systematically replaced references to God and the saints with the Goddess and an assortment of Pagan divinities.

There are still, as of this writing, a number of occult orders that continue to work within the Christian magical tradition. Notable are occult Christian bodies drawing on the lineages of independent bishops, a number of English magical orders with a comfortable relationship with the Anglican Church, and the system of focused contemplative prayer, using the ancient name of theurgy, which evolved in nineteenth-century French occult circles and is still practiced in a variety of countries. *SEE* THEURGY. Churches and other religious bodies with a Gnostic focus have moved in this direction as well, buoyed by the soaring interest in Gnosticism set off by the translation of the Nag Hammadi scriptures; *SEE* GNOSTICISM.

Corpus Hermeticum: A collection of fifteen treatises attributed to Hermes Trismegistus, originally written in Egypt at some point between the first and third centuries of the Common Era. The surviving set of treatises is only a small part of what was once a very large literature produced by Egyptian Hermeticists. *SEE* HERMETICISM.

After the triumph of Christianity in the Mediterranean world and the suppression of Pagan religious traditions, the *Corpus Hermeticum* survived in a few collections in the Byzantine Empire, which retained enough interest in Neoplatonist philosophy to value it. A copy is known to have been in the possession of the Greek Neoplatonist Michael Psellus.

Around 1460, a copy of the *Corpus Hermeticum* was obtained by one of the agents of Cosimo de Medici, ruler of Florence, who was amassing western Europe's largest library of Greek works. When this copy came to Cosimo's attention in 1463, he asked Marsilio Ficino—the young head of Florence's Platonic Academy, then about to start work on the first Latin translation of the complete works of Plato—to put Plato aside and translate Hermes first. The translation was finished in 1464, and became an immediate bestseller by the standards of the time, going through sixteen editions before the end of the sixteenth century. This popularity was in part the result of a mistake in dating. Until 1614, when Isaac Casaubon demonstrated the real date of the treatises on linguistic grounds, scholars across Europe believed that the Hermetic writings dated from far more ancient times. Hermes Trismegistus himself was usually thought to be a contemporary of Moses, and thus the first philosopher and theologian in human history. Hermetic writings were cited by a number of early Christian writers, including Lactantius and Augustine, who accepted the same early date. During the century and a half after Ficino's translation was published, therefore, educated Europeans saw the *Corpus Hermeticum* as nothing less than the oldest wisdom in the world. The magical doctrines included in the treatises thus played a major role in laying the foundation for the Renaissance magical synthesis.

The great popularity of the *Corpus Hermeticum* came to an end in 1614 with the publication of a detailed study of its origins by Isaac Casaubon (1559–1614), a Swiss Protestant scholar living in England. (It is an interesting detail that his son, Meric Casaubon, carried on the family tradition of hostility to occultism and was responsible for publishing the diaries of John Dee's angelic workings in an attempt to discredit the great Elizabethan magus.) Casaubon pointed out that the treatises mention the Greek sculptor Phidias and the Pythian games, quote from many Greek authors dating from long after Hermes' supposed lifetime, and are written in a late style of Greek using words that do not appear until Christian times.

Casaubon's conclusions were almost universally accepted at the time and, with some modifications, are still accepted by scholars today. A few stalwart Hermeticists such as Robert Fludd dismissed or denied Casaubon's arguments, but with very little effect. The Hermetic treatises received very little attention until recent times, when the writings of historians such as Frances Yates pointed out their importance to the history of magic, and a small but significant number of modern magicians began to include Hermetic materials in their work. *SEE ALSO* HERMES TRISMEGISTUS.

Crowley, Aleister: (Edward Alexander Crowley) English writer, occultist, Antichrist, and self-proclaimed messiah of the New Aeon, 1875–1947. Easily the most controversial figure in the recent history of Western occultism, Crowley was born into the Plymouth Brethren, a small and deeply puritanical Protestant sect that originated most of modern Fundamentalist Christian theology. His father, a wealthy brewer, died when Crowley was five years old, leaving him to be raised by his mother and uncle. He had an excellent (and expensive) public school education and went to Trinity College, Cambridge, where he dabbled in chemistry but left without taking a degree.

While at college, he wrote and self-published his first books, a collection of philosophical poetry titled *Aceldama* and a volume of pornographic verse titled *White Stains*. Upon encountering a copy of A. E. Waite's *Book of Black Magic and of Pacts*, however, his interests turned to the occult, and in 1898 he was initiated into the Hermetic Order of the Golden Dawn. As a member of the order, he studied with the occultist and Buddhist Allan Bennett (1872–1923), but was denied advancement to the Adeptus Minor grade and the order's inner magical teachings because the senior adepts of the order in London disapproved of his behavior. The order's chief, Samuel Liddell Mathers (1854–1918), proceeded to initiate him into the Adeptus Minor grade in Paris, an act that helped bring about the schism in the order in 1900. During the schism Crowley remained loyal to Mathers and acted as the chief's emissary, although his inept handling of his mission and his insistence on parading about in full Highland dress through the whole affair did not help Mathers' cause.

Crowley's lifestyle at this time was still fueled by his inherited money, and he traveled widely, went on mountain climbing expeditions, and devoted much of his time to chess, poetry, and a variety of sexual liaisons. It is entirely in character that he paid the chef of a London hotel to name a dish after him, *sole à lá Crowley*, and commissioned Augustus John—the most prestigious portraitist of the time—to paint his portrait.

In 1903 he married Rose Kelly, the daughter of a portrait painter, and took her on a world tour by way of a honeymoon. The next year, while in Cairo, he received—according to his account, via a disembodied but clearly audible voice—a communication from a spirit named Aiwass, who claimed to be the representative of the spiritual powers governing the next age of world history, the Aeon of Horus. Over a three-day period, Aiwass dictated to Crowley the text of *Liber AL vel Legis*, the Book of the Law, and proclaimed Crowley the Beast 666 from the Book of Revelation.

Thereafter, as his marriage disintegrated and his literary career ground to a halt, Crowley's involvement in magic became steadily more intense, and he gradually became convinced of the accuracy of Aiwass' message and his own messianic role. With the last of his inherited money, he founded and ran a lavish magazine—*The Equinox*—devoted to the occult. In its pages, he published many of the Golden Dawn papers and brought them for the first time to the attention of the broader occult community. A variety of intensive magical workings, alone or with others, convinced him that he was working his way up the grades of magical attainment. He also accepted initiation into the Ordo Templi Orientis, a small quasi-Masonic organization run by a dubious character named Theodor Reuss, and went on to take over large parts of the order and reshape it to fit his philosophy.

At the outbreak of World War I he moved to the United States, where he supported himself by journalism, pursued his magical training, and involved himself in the politics of the American occult scene. In 1920 he and a small group of followers moved to Cefalu, in Sicily, where they established what would now be called a commune and devoted their time to sex, magic, and drugs. There Crowley went through an experience that, in his opinion, marked his ascent to the grade of Ipsissimus, the highest level of magical attainment. Shortly thereafter Raoul Loveday, one of the community's members, died of food poisoning. The result was a public scandal in Great Britain and Italy, and the Italian dictator Mussolini ordered Crowley expelled from the country.

After the collapse of the Cefalu community, Crowley spent a while in Tunisia and France, becoming a heroin addict in the process, and finally returned to England. Not long after his return, he happened to read a passage in the autobiography of British sculptor Nina Hammett that referred to him as a "black magician." Crowley reacted by suing her for libel. Unfortunately for him, British libel law required her to prove the accuracy of her statement in order to defend herself. This she did, in the eyes of the jury, the press, and the public, in a sensational trial that left Crowley's reputation and finances in shreds.

Crowley spent the remainder of his life in cheap lodgings, first in London and later in Hastings, on the Sussex coast, corresponding with a small circle of students and scrambling to support his drug habit. While rumors in the occult community have claimed for decades that he was hired to write the original Wiccan Book of Shadows by Gerald Gardner, there is no evidence that this is true, and a good deal of evidence that Gardner wrote it himself after Crowley's demise. On Crowley's death, his estate was valued at fourteen shillings.

degree: In fraternal and magical lodge systems, levels of initiation, each of which has its own ceremony, symbolism, and traditional lore. The term "grades" is also used with the same meaning.

The system of degrees was originally inspired by the three-level structure of the medieval guild system, in which a member could expect to pass through the stages of apprentice, journeyman, and master in the course of his career. Apprentices were taught the basics of a craft in exchange for room and board, and were bound to work for a master for a fixed period of years. Journeymen, companions, or fellows—the terms for this stage varied—had completed an apprenticeship and worked for masters for wages, developing their skills in the guild's trade. Upon completion of a "master piece"—an item of work that showed complete mastery of the craft—journeymen advanced to the rank of master, gained voting rights in the guild, and took on apprentices and journeymen of their own.

This same three-level structure was used by the operative stonemasons' guilds that turned into Freemasonry,
and gave rise to the Masonic degree structure of Entered
Apprentice, Fellow Craft, and Master Mason. Many other
groups that borrowed Masonic methods took on versions
of the same system, and a three-degree structure of initiations is still the most common both in fraternal lodges and
in magical ones. It has also been adopted into Wicca and
Druidry, along with a surprising amount of Masonic symbolism and terminology.

Later, with the development of additional Masonic
degrees, more elaborate degree structures made their appearance. The most extravagant example is the ninety-nine
degrees of the Masonic Rite of Memphis and Mizraim, although very few of these degrees were ever developed beyond a very basic framework. In the Masonic Scottish Rite
of thirty-three degrees, on the other hand, every degree
has its own fully developed ritual, symbolism, and teachings. Other systems, some modeled on Masonry and others
deriving from different sources, have different degree structures, although none seem to have attempted the complex-
ity of these latter Masonic systems. One worth mentioning is the Golden Dawn system of twelve grades, based on
the Cabalistic Tree of Life, which is itself derived from an
older Rosicrucian scheme of nine grades used by the German Order of the Gold and Rosy Cross. Another is that of
the Independent Order of Odd Fellows (IOOF), the larg-

est non-Masonic fraternal order, which has a total of ten degrees of initiation divided into three levels, and has influenced a number of American occult orders. The nine-degree structure of the Ordo Templi Orientis (OTO) has also been much copied over the last century; *SEE* LODGE, MAGICAL.

Eastern Star, Order of the: An auxiliary of American Freemasonry, the Order of the Eastern Star admits Master Masons and women connected to them by birth or marriage. Christian, charitable, and utterly proper, it has nothing at all to do with the occult, but its emblem—an inverted pentagram bearing an assortment of symbols, and letters spelling the word FATAL—has caused a good deal of confusion and suspicion. FATAL stands for the sentence "Fairest Among Ten thousand, Altogether Lovely," which may give some sense of the order's general flavor. *SEE* FREEMASONRY.

Egyptian occultism: From the time of the pharaohs to the present, ancient Egypt has had a reputation as the homeland of magic par excellence. A proverb from the Talmud claims that all the magic in the world is divided into ten parts; Egypt got nine, and the rest of the world split up the one remaining part. Similar comments can be found throughout ancient, medieval, and early modern literature.

Many Western occult systems, including some with roots very far from the banks of the Nile, trace themselves back to alleged Egyptian origins. While most of these accounts are mythic rather than historical, and some are fairly straightforward examples of fakery, there is a core of truth behind them: to a very large degree, the Western occult tradition itself began in the country its ancient inhabitants called Khem, "the Black Land."

The origins of ancient Egyptian civilization are traced by modern archeologists to 4000 BCE, rooted in tribal cultures that were established along the banks of the Nile for many centuries before that time. By 3200 BCE, a plethora of small kingdoms had given way to two—Lower Egypt, comprising the Nile Delta, and Upper Egypt, extending south from the beginning of the delta to the First Cataract near Aswan. The two kingdoms were united by Narmer, the founder of the First Dynasty. By the Third Dynasty, the first pyramids were being built, and much of ancient Egyptian civilization was already solidly in place. That civilization persisted through some thirty dynasties reaching from 3200 BCE to the first centuries of the Common Era, when the impact of Roman rule, the coming of Christianity, and finally the arrival of Islam brought it to an end.

Magic was pervasive throughout Egyptian religion, philosophy, and daily life. For example, part of the daily temple liturgy to the sun god Re—performed in temples throughout Egypt from Middle Kingdom times onward— used a wax "voodoo doll" of Re's great enemy, the underworld serpent Apophis. The Apophis figure was impaled with copper knives and then burned, to vanquish the serpent and assist Re in his voyage through the heavens. At the same time, the priests performing this rite also sacrificed other wax figures, who stood for the political and military enemies of the reigning pharaoh; they also offered still more figures, representing the personal enemies of the donors who paid for the ritual's daily performance. Separating out "religion" from "magic" in a ceremony of this sort is a futile process, as the ancient Egyptians themselves drew no such distinction. Although there is an Egyptian word for magic—*heka*—there is no ancient Egyptian term that can be translated as "religion."

The primary practitioners of magic in ancient Egypt, in fact, were the temple priests themselves. Surviving records from pharaonic through Ptolemaic times show no sign of a separate class of magicians, of the sort found in most other ancient and modern societies. Instead, the priesthoods themselves worked magic. Magical practices were an important part of the *seshtau*, "that which is hidden"—the inner rituals of the temple cult, which were enacted in the inner sanctuaries of Egyptian temples.

Except for those at the very top of the hierarchy, Egyptian priests served at the temples in rotation, and performed ritual workings for private clients in the intervals between periods of temple duty. It's indicative that the standard late Egyptian word for "magician," *hariteb*, is descended from the older phrase *hari-hebhari-tep*, "chief lector priest," an important Egyptian priestly rank. (The same Egyptian word gave rise to the biblical Hebrew word *hartum*, a common Old Testament term for "magician.")

The Egyptian word for magic, *heka*, was also the name of a god—Heka, "Magic" or "the Magician," who had shrines in the Egyptian cities of Heliopolis and Memphis, and a festival on the twenty-second day of the month of Athyr. Coffin texts from the Old Kingdom describe Heka as the first creation of the primordial god Atum. Later texts describe him as the ka or vital spirit of the solar god Re, traveling in Re's sunboat and helping him vanquish the evil serpent Apophis. Other gods and goddesses also claimed the title *werethekau*, "great of magic," and the Tenth Dynasty text "Instructions for King Merikare" includes magic as one of the great gifts—together with Heaven, Earth, air, food, and good government—that the gods had given to human beings.

As the place of pharaoh's enemies in the ritual against Apep shows, magical practices were an important part of the political structure. Magical operations against Egypt's military and political opponents were a common event. Ritual "execration figures"—that is, small statues of domestic and foreign enemies of the state—were used in a variety of magical practices, and the pharaohs even had such figures painted on their sandals, so they could symbolically trample their enemies with each step. (A pair of such sandals were found in the tomb of Tutankhamen.)

Cursing ceremonies were also much used against opponents of the Egyptian state; these included the *Sed deseruor*, "Breaking of the Red Vases," in which pottery vessels were inscribed with the names of intended targets and then shattered, and the custom of writing letters to the dead, who were asked either to carry out various activities themselves or to appeal to the gods on the magician's behalf. This latter method seems to have been ancestral to the later Greek and Roman use of *defixiones*, or binding tablets.

The same practices were also turned against the regime on occasion. When Queen Tiye, one of the wives of Rameses III, set out to murder her husband by magic and put her son on the throne, the ritual scrolls used in the plot were stolen from the pharaoh's own library. Not all Egyptian magic had such hostile intentions behind it.

Healing magic was much practiced, especially for victims of scorpion stings and snakebite, and overlapped considerably with the abundant lore of ancient Egyptian medicine and surgery. A great deal of magic also found a place in the elaborate rituals for the dead, and texts such as the *Pert em Hru*, or "Book of Coming Forth by Day," the so-called Egyptian Book of the Dead, are important repositories of magical ritual.

The impact of Egyptian magical traditions on the other peoples of the ancient world was considerable. During the last period of Egyptian independence, the Saite period (663–525 BCE), the political and military alliance between Egypt and the city-states of Greece made it possible for a number of Greek intellectuals, Pythagoras foremost among them, to study Egyptian temple lore; *SEE* PYTHAGORAS. The Persian invasion of 525 BCE closed off this option, but Alexander the Great's conquest of Egypt in 332 BCE opened the door wide again and ushered in the Ptolemaic period, a span of three centuries in which a Greek-Egyptian hybrid culture came into being on the banks of the Nile. During this period, the Egyptian city of Alexandria became a center of Greek culture and philosophy, and several important currents of Greek thought absorbed a significant amount from Egyptian sources. In particular, the Pythagorean tradition—itself rooted in Egyptian soil—flourished under the Ptolemies, and the foundations of Neoplatonism were also laid in Alexandrian philosophical circles. The fusion between Greek and Egyptian culture extended far enough that Egyptian priests could and did become Greek philosophers as well. It was also in Alexandria during the same period that alchemy first appeared in the Western world.

The Roman conquest in 30 BCE marked the beginning of the end for ancient Egyptian culture. While the Roman government was willing to permit many Egyptian religious practices to continue, anything that strayed too close to what Romans understood as magic ran into increasing legal difficulties. Edicts of 199 and 359 CE prohibited the traditional *peheneter* oracles, and all magical practices were forbidden by imperial legislation starting in the time of Augustus and frequently renewed by his successors. In response, Egyptian priests carried on their more obviously magical practices in secret, and a class of full-time magicians operating on the far side of the law began to emerge.

It was in this context that ritual texts from the ancient temple lore made their way into the assortment of spellbooks from Roman Egypt now known as the Graeco-Egyptian magical papyri. The same forces shaped the Hermetic and Gnostic movements, which fused Egyptian ritual, Greek philosophy, and Hebrew theology into a religious approach that replaced much of what remained of the moribund temple traditions. On a more intellectual level, the diffusion of Egyptian temple lore into late classical magic had a potent influence on Neoplatonist philosophy, and became a central factor in the theurgic Neoplatonism of Iamblichus and Proclus. *SEE* HERMETICISM; PLATONISM; THEURGY.

The new, secretive magical spirituality proved both more durable and easier to export beyond Egypt's borders. When the last Egyptian temples went out of existence in the fifth century, it remained for these later systems to carry on what remained of Egypt's magical legacy.

electional astrology: The art of choosing the most favorable time for events using astrological cycles. Electional astrology is essentially ordinary astrology turned upside down. Instead of starting with a given time and place, and working out the astrological factors in play then and there, the electional astrologer starts out with a set of desired astrological factors and sets out to find a time and place when those factors are present. For example, a marriage might be scheduled for a time when Venus is strong and in positive aspects. Electional astrology can range from relatively simple approaches up to exhaustive calculations involving many factors. Many of the complexities involve using the birth chart of the person seeking to plan the event, and working out a time when the planets and signs are in placements that not only favor the event in question, but also harmonize with the person's birth chart. In the case of a wedding, in turn, both spouses' charts need to be taken into account.

Electional astrology has been in common use since ancient times. It played an important role in society in the Middle Ages and Renaissance, when few significant events would be planned without the advice of an astrologer. While the decline of astrology at the time of the Scientific Revolution affected electional astrology at least as much as any other branch of the art, it has staged an impressive comeback in the last century and is actively studied and pursued by many astrologers today. Electional astrology also has a direct application to magical practice. Traditional textbooks of magic such as the *Key of Solomon* and H. Cornelius Agrippa's *Three Books of Occult Philosophy* routinely instruct the magician to do certain rituals at times chosen for astrological reasons. For example, Agrippa instructs the magician to make a magical ring to bring prophetic dreams when either the sun or Saturn is in the ninth house, favorably aspected, and in the sign that was in the ascendant in the birth chart of the person for whom the ring is made. In medieval and Renaissance magic, this sort of electional astrology was the most common way to calculate the proper time of a magical ritual, and some magicians still use this method at present. *SEE* CEREMONIAL MAGIC. *SEE ALSO* ASTROLOGY.

Fama Fraternitatis: (Latin, "report of the brotherhood") The commonly used short form of the title of the first Rosicrucian manifesto. *SEE* ROSICRUCIANS.

Fludd, Robert: English physician and occultist, 1574–1637. The son of a government official turned country squire, Fludd was born and grew up in rural Kent, and entered Oxford University in 1592, receiving his bachelor's degree in 1596 and his master's in 1598. After the latter, he traveled in Europe for six years, working as a tutor for aristocratic families in France and Italy. During these travels, he became interested in medicine, and when he returned to Oxford in 1604 he began formal medical studies, graduating with a doctorate in 1605. After some initial troubles with the College of Physicians, the medical trade organization in Britain at the time, he was admitted to practice in 1609 and began a successful medical career.

In addition to medicine, though, Fludd had a lifelong interest in astrology, occult philosophy, and Cabala, and also made important contributions to the Art of Memory; SEE ART OF MEMORY. In his undergraduate days he was already good enough at astrology to identify a thief by means of a horary chart; SEE HORARY ASTROLOGY. Later he mastered geomancy as well, and nearly got into serious trouble during his European travels when a group of Jesuits found out about his divinations and went to the papal vice-legate, a high church official, in an attempt to get Fludd arrested. The vice-legate, however, turned out to be just as interested in geomancy as Fludd, and invited the Englishman to dinner, where they spent a pleasant evening discussing the art.

After his return to England and the beginning of his medical career, Fludd launched what would be his great contribution to Western occultism, a massive encyclopedia of all human knowledge from the perspective of Renaissance occult philosophy. The first volume of *Utriusque Cosmi Maioris scilicet et Minoris Metaphysica, Physica et Technica Historia* (*Metaphysical, Physical and Technical History of Both Universes, that is, the Greater and the Lesser*) was published by Johann Theodor de Bry in 1617, and further volumes followed over the next few years.

A prolific writer and vigorous debater, Fludd was active in pamphlet debates (the Renaissance equivalent of

modern Internet flamewars) with proponents of materialist science, such as the French priest Marin Mersenne
and the English physician William Foster. He never quite
finished the great encyclopedia, publishing several important books of Hermetic medicine and spagyric alchemy in
the later part of his life. He died peacefully at his home in
1637 and was buried at the Fludd family parish church in
Bearstead, Kent. *SEE ALSO* HERMETICISM.

Freemasonry: The Order of Free and Accepted Masons
is an international fraternal order with massive historical
connections to occultism. While not actually an occult
organization, Freemasonry is the most important of the
fraternal orders in the Western world, and the source of
a very large percentage of occult ideas about lodges, de
grees, initiations, symbolism, and the like. In its basic and
essential form, Freemasonry consists of three degrees of
initiation that draw their symbolism and teachings from
the stonemason's trade, and from the biblical account of
the building of King Solomon's Temple. On this relatively
simple foundation has been raised an immense structure
of ritual, symbolism, philosophy, magic, philanthropy,
spirituality, speculation, and sheer hogwash.

The origins of Freemasonry are wrapped in a thick fog
of guesswork and wishful thinking. Masonic historians,
at various points over the last three hundred years, have

traced the origins of Freemasonry to ancient Egyptian priests, Roman colleges of architecture, and the medieval Knights Templar, as well as to King Solomon's Temple itself. *SEE* TEMPLE OF SOLOMON. Many of these claims can still be found in popular literature today. There is, however, no actual evidence that any of these groups had anything to do with the historical origins of Freemasonry. Rather, the evidence of current research suggests that its roots can be found in the much more prosaic realm of late medieval stonemasons' guilds in Scotland and England.

Scottish records of working stonemasons' lodges provide the oldest known references to the Mason Word (the secret method of identifying oneself as a Mason to other Masons), permanent masons' lodges, multiple degrees of initiation, and the initiation of people who were not working stonemasons into lodges. As late as 1691, the Rev. Robert Kirk referred to the Mason Word as one of five "curiosities" common in Scotland but rare or nonexistent elsewhere. There is also documentary evidence that Scottish stonemasons were expected to study the Art of Memory as of 1599, the date of statutes issued by William Schaw, Master of Works to the King of Scotland. This points to a familiarity with traditions of Hermetic imagery that later played a central role in Masonic ritual and practice. *SEE* ART OF MEMORY.

These traditions, and the symbolic and ceremonial dimensions that ultimately became the core of the Masonic movement, took their place gradually over at least a century. In the early seventeenth century, most members of Mason's lodges were operative masons—that is, working men who made their living in the building trades. Starting around 1640, men who had no business connection to building, but were interested in the masons' rituals and symbols, began to join lodges; they were called accepted masons. By 1700, accepted masons were in the majority in most lodges, and there were many lodges without a single member who had ever spread mortar with a trowel. In 1717, four London lodges came together to form the Grand Lodge of England (now the United Grand Lodge of England), the oldest Grand Lodge in Freemasonry. The next hundred years were a period of explosive growth, as lodges were founded throughout Britain, Europe, and the American colonies as well.

During this time Masonry became entangled in the complex net of political and magical intrigues surrounding the House of Stuart, which was driven off the British throne in 1688 and tried for most of a century to regain its former place. The Jacobites, as the pro-Stuart party was called, used the secrecy of Masonic lodges as a shield for their conspiracies against the House of Hanover, the new British royal house. The Hanoverian side responded in kind. The Grand Lodge of England, which was a stronghold of Hanoverian Masons, and the Scottish Rite, which developed out of Jacobite lodges in France, both took shape in the midst of these controversies.

Central to these intrigues was Scottish Freemason Andrew Michael Ramsay (1686–1743), a Jacobite and Catholic convert who spent most of his life in exile in France. In the 1730s, as part of the preparations for the Stuart rising of 1745, Ramsay played a central role in creating a new, more complex system of "Scottish" Freemasonry closely allied to the Jacobite cause, and heavily loaded with Hermetic and occult material, in keeping with Ramsay's own interests. After Ramsay's death and the failure of the 1745 rising, Scottish Freemasonry regrouped into a Rite of Perfection of twenty-five degrees, which later evolved into the Scottish Rite of thirty-three degrees.

Another set of complexities emerged out of the relations between Freemasonry and the Catholic Church. These started off poorly and rapidly worsened. Anything associated with Protestant England was looked at suspiciously in Rome, and as Masonry spread in France and Italy, it drew most of its members from liberal circles whom supported political reform and religious toleration—two things the church was not prepared to accept. The first Catholic condemnation of Masonry, the papal bull *In Eminente*, was promulgated in 1732, and followed by others. To this day a Catholic who becomes a Mason risks excommunication. The Catholic condemnation of Freemasonry has at times risen to the level of claiming that Masonry is actually a front for the deliberate worship of Satan, a charge that has involved the church in extreme embarrassment at least once already in its history.

Despite the tide of Catholic rhetoric, and more recent flurries of criticism from fundamentalist Protestants who have become convinced that Masonry is somehow connected to secular humanism and the Antichrist, the reality of the Masonic lodge is prosaic enough. Lodges hold business meetings for third-degree members at intervals ranging from once each week to once each month, usually with a dinner either before or after the meeting; perform traditional and rather verbose initiation rituals for new members; raise money to donate to a wide range of worthy causes; and behave like most other clubs. On initiation, members promise to keep the rituals, identification signals, and private business of the lodge secret from nonmembers, to follow the various rules and bylaws of the lodge and the order, and to maintain standards of good behavior with other Masons. The tone of the whole system can be measured adequately by the fact that an open Bible is part of the lodge furnishings, and the Pledge of Allegiance is recited by American Freemasons at the beginning of each meeting.

The degrees of initiation conferred in Freemasonry fall into two broad classes. The first, the Symbolic or "Blue Lodge" degrees, are the foundation of the entire system, and any person who has received them is considered to be fully initiated as a Freemason. They are:

1°: Entered Apprentice
2°: Fellow Craft
3°: Master Mason

Beyond this, matters get confusing very quickly. There are higher Masonic grades, assembled in a variety of rites, and there are also concordant bodies with their own degrees, which are not considered Masonic but which recruit members only among Master Masons. In the United States, two main rites—the York Rite and the Scottish Rite—attract most Masons interested in higher degrees, but other rites exist, and concordant bodies number in the dozens. None of these additional rites or bodies have any authority over the Blue Lodges that work the three degrees already mentioned. The York Rite in North America offers the following degrees, divided up into three sets:

Chapter degrees
    Mark Master
    Past Master
    Most Excellent Master
    Royal Arch

Cryptic degrees
>   Royal Master
>   Select Master
>   Super Excellent Master

Knights Templar degrees
>   Order of the Red Cross
>   Order of the Knights of Malta
>   Order of Knights Templar

For its part, the Scottish Rite provides its initiates with a much more extensive set of degrees. The following degrees are offered in the Southern Jurisdiction of the Ancient and Accepted Scottish Rite, which includes most of the United States:

Lodge of Perfection degrees
>   4°: Secret Master
>   5°: Perfect Master
>   6°: Intimate Secretary
>   7°: Provost and Judge
>   8°: Intendant of the Building
>   9°: Elu of the Nine
>   10°: Elu of the Fifteen
>   11°: Elu of the Twelve
>   12°: Master Architect
>   13°: Royal Arch of Solomon
>   14°: Perfect Elu

Chapter of Rose Croix degrees

  15°: Knight of the East, of the Sword, or of the Eagle

  16°: Prince of Jerusalem

  17°: Knight of the East and West

  18°: Knight of the Rose Croix

Council of Kadosh degrees

  19°: Pontiff

  20°: Master of the Symbolic Lodge

  21°: Noachite or Prussian Knight

  22°: Knight Royal Axe, Prince of Libanus

  23°: Chief of the Tabernacle

  24°: Prince of the Tabernacle

  25°: Knight of the Brazen Serpent

  26°: Prince of Mercy or Scottish Trinitarian

  27°: Knight Commander of the Temple

  28°: Knight of the Sun or Prince Adept

  29°: Scottish Knight of Saint Andrew

  30°: Knight Kadosh or Knight of the White and Black
      Eagle

Consistory degrees

  31°: Inspector Inquisitor

  32°: Master of the Royal Secret

Supreme Council degree

  33°: Sovereign Grand Inspector General

Many of these Scottish Rite degrees have fairly explicit occult content, and Albert Pike, who was responsible for creating much of the present Scottish Rite system, expounded that system in occult terms in his massive *Morals and Dogma of the Ancient and Accepted Scottish Rite* (1871); SEE PIKE, ALBERT. Nonetheless, very few Scottish Rite Masons pay much attention to this aspect of the system, and there seems to be no reason to think that the present leaders of the Scottish Rite are occult adepts—or, for that matter, occultists at all.

The internal politics among the various Masonic bodies are extremely complex, involving overlapping jurisdictions, disputes as to who is or is not a valid Mason, and the like. There are also bodies such as Co-Masonry, a Masonic order open to women as well as men, which nearly all other Masonic bodies refuse to recognize, and Adoptive Masonry, open only to women, which has a complex relationship to the male only Masonic Lodges. SEE LODGE, MAGICAL.

gematria: The art of Cabalistic numerology, a system for analyzing Hebrew (and other) words by way of the numerical value of the letters of the Hebrew alphabet. Hebrew (like Greek and many other ancient languages) uses what is called an isopsephic alphabet—that is, an alphabet in which letters also stand for numbers. Where modern people write down numbers or do arithmetic using Arabic numerals (1, 2, 3, and so on), ancient and medieval Jews used letters of the Hebrew alphabet—Aleph for 1, Beth for 2, and so on.

In the hands of Cabalists, this habit became a tool for subtle analyses of the scriptures. For instance, there is a scene in the story of the patriarch Abraham, in Genesis 18:2, in which three "men" come to visit him. They are representatives of God, and bring tidings that he and his wife Sarah will have a son. The passage starts off in Hebrew, *Ve-hineh shelshah* . . . ("And behold, three . . ."). The letters of this phrase, added up, equal 701. The sentence

Elu Michael Raphael ve-Raphael ("These are Michael, Raphael, and Gabriel") also adds up to 701, and this has been used for centuries as a way of showing who the three "men" were.

This tool predictably led in some strange directions. For example, NChSh, *nachash*, "serpent," is equal to 358; so is MShICh, "messiah." On this basis some Cabalists argued that the serpent of the Garden of Eden was in some sense the Messiah—a suggestion that the Gnostics made a long time earlier. Equally odd is the equation that links *Qadosh ha-Qadoshim*, "Holy of Holies," the name of the inner chamber in the Temple of Jerusalem, and *Eisheth Zenunim*, "Woman of Whoredom," the archdemon of prostitution in Hebrew demonology; both phrases add up to 1,424. Equations like these have led more cautious Cabalists to point out that while gematria can reveal truths, it can also lead to remarkable nonsense, and should be used with care and common sense. *SEE ALSO* ARITHMANCY; CABALA.

Gnosticism: (from Greek *gnosis*," knowledge") Any of a set of wildly diverse spiritual traditions that emerged in the ancient world around the beginning of the Common Era. Their exact origins are the subject of violent disputes among modern scholars, but Greek mystical traditions, Zoroastrian dualism from Persia, Jewish teachings, and early Christian ideas may all have played some part in generating the Gnostic movement.

Their history is difficult to trace, since Gnosticism was violently opposed by the Christian church. Except for a collection of Gnostic scriptures recovered from Nag Hammadi in Egypt, nearly all the information we now have about Gnosticism thus comes from its bitter enemies. It is clear, though, that Gnostic sects were in existence in much of the Roman world by the second century of the Common Era, flourished in the third and early fourth centuries, and were eliminated or driven underground in the late fourth and fifth centuries.

The core theme uniting all Gnostic teachings is that of *gnosis*, "knowledge," which is not a matter of ordinary learning but a personal experience of spiritual truth. The Gnostic is not interested in belief; he or she wants to know, directly and personally, the spiritual realities of the cosmos. Most Gnostic systems combine this stress on personal experience with a harshly dualistic and at least slightly paranoid vision of the universe. In this view, the entire material world is a prison created by evil powers, the archons, to entrap souls from a higher world of light. To be living in a material body in the world is to be trapped in an alien realm, at the mercy of the archons and their terrifying leader—the "blind god" Ialdabaoth, also known as Saklas and Samael, who is also the God of the Old Testament.

Beyond the false world of matter lies the true world, the world of light, ruled by the aeons, who are both beings and realms. The creation of the material world and the archons was considered by many Gnostics to be the result of a mistake by one of the aeons, Sophia ("Wisdom"), who desired to create something on her own, and managed only to give birth to a maimed, blind entity, shaped like a serpent with a lion's head: Ialdabaoth. Hoping to hide her deed from the other aeons, Sophia cast her creation out of the world of light into the void. In the process, though, sparks of light from the true world entered the void, and when Ialdabaoth fashioned a world out of the substance of the void, the sparks were trapped in it. Ialdabaoth created the other archons; together they made physical bodies as prisons for the sparks of light, and created stars and planets to enmesh the sparks in a merciless net of astrological destiny. In this way the world we know came into being.

The goal of most versions of Gnosticism is to break free of Ialdabaoth's world and return to the world of light. This escape hatch is not open to all, however. Many Gnostic sources divide human beings into three classes: hylics (from *hyle*, "matter") who are robotic creations of the archons, and cannot escape the material world; psychics (from *psyche*, "mind") who have the potential to break free from matter and rise to the realm of light, but have to work at it; and pneumatics (from *pneuma*, "spirit") who have gnosis as an innate birthright and can count on returning to the world of light. These basic principles seem to have been accepted by most (although not all) Gnostic systems as a common foundation. The structures built on that foundation, however, were fantastically diverse. Some Gnostic traditions were explicitly Christian, and taught that Jesus of Nazareth was an aeon of the world of light who descended into the false world of matter to liberate souls from the clutches of the Archons. Others pointed to Seth, the third son of Adam, as the one who opened the way of escape. Other Gnostics turned the villains of the Bible—Cain, Esau, the inhabitants of Sodom, and so forth—into heroes rebelling against the power of the evil creator.

There were a few Gnostic teachers and traditions that ignored the Bible and the imagery of standard Judeo-Christian thought altogether. Most Gnostic writings, however, kept a focus on these sources, reinterpreting them in various ways. To some extent, Gnosticism functioned as a sort of conspiracy theory of the spiritual realm, treating orthodox ideas as a theological "official account" that had to be seen through in order to get at the truth. Gnostic writers combed through the events of the Book of Genesis, in particular, in much the same way that modern conspiracy buffs pore over details of the Kennedy assassination—and their proposed interpretations varied just as widely.

Gnostic practice was as diverse as Gnostic theory. Magical rites were apparently much practiced; Plotinus, the great Platonist philosopher, criticizes their reliance on charms in his essay *Against the Gnostics*. A number of the surviving Gnostic scriptures include magical invocations and words of power closely related to those found in the Graeco-Egyptian magical papyri.

There were some Gnostics who argued in favor of a life of asceticism and spiritual discipline, and sex in particular was often roundly condemned, since it created new human bodies in which souls were imprisoned. Others argued that if the god of conventional religion was evil, what he prohibited must be good, and on this basis insisted that every kind of sexual activity was permitted. One middle ground between these positions was to prohibit forms of lovemaking that could lead to pregnancy but to consider anything else fair game.

After its suppression in the Roman world, Gnosticism continued to be taught and practiced in small underground sects in various parts of the Middle East. At least one of these sects, the Mandeans, has survived in southern Iraq to this day. Another, the Bogomils, flourished in the early Middle Ages in what is now Bulgaria, and missionaries from this sect traveled west to Italy and southern France in the twelfth and thirteenth centuries, launching the most widely known Gnostic movement in the West, the Cathar heresy.

The Inquisition, formally established in 1239 as a weapon against Catharism, gradually eliminated what was left of the Cathars after the church-sponsored crusade that began in 1208. Gnosticism in the Western world thereafter existed primarily as a footnote in history books until the nineteenth century, when several small Gnostic sects were established in France as part of the early phases of the occult renaissance of that period. Attitudes toward the Gnostics underwent a major change around that time, as part of the Romantic revaluation of outcast traditions and rejected knowledge. Many opponents of established versions of Christianity turned to Gnosticism, either as a polemic weapon or as a framework for new quasi-Christian approaches to spirituality. The Theosophical Society, which spearheaded the alternative spirituality movement in the late nineteenth and early twentieth centuries, portrayed the Gnostics as enlightened mystics slaughtered by bigoted orthodox fanatics; this portrayal became widespread throughout occult circles during the "Theosophical century" from 1875 to 1975. Swiss psychologist Carl Jung (1875–1961) also drew substantially on what was known of Gnosticism in his creation of analytic psychology; *SEE* JUNG, CARL GUSTAV.

It is worth noting, however, that all speculation and discussion of Gnosticism from the fall of Rome until the early 1970s was based on a handful of sources, nearly all of them written by early Christian clergymen who were far more interested in denouncing the Gnostics than understanding them. In 1945, however, farmers near the village of Nag Hammadi in Egypt came across a buried pottery jar in which were concealed twelve leather-bound volumes of ancient Gnostic scriptures. Scholarly turf wars delayed their publication and translation for more than two decades, but a complete facsimile edition was published in stages between 1972 and 1977, and a one-volume English translation was issued in 1977.

The result has been a great upsurge in interest in Gnosticism, and the rise and spread of a number of Gnostic religious and spiritual organizations. Several alternative branches of Christianity connected with the independent bishops movement have redefined themselves as Gnostic. Few of these recent Gnostics, though, have ventured into the profound dualism of ancient Gnostic thought—which may be just as well. *SEE ALSO* CHRISTIAN OCCULTISM; HERMETICISM; PLATONISM.

gold: The most valuable of the metals known to the ancients, gold is usually assigned to the sun and put to use in solar talismans and other magical devices. Cabalists generally assign it to Tiphareth, the sixth Sephirah of the Tree of Life, although a minority assign it to the fifth Sephirah, Geburah. *SEE* CABALA.

The creation of gold from mercury or some other less valuable metal is one of the central goals of alchemy. Some alchemical texts, however, warn that "our gold is not the common gold," and references to gold in alchemical sources and other occult writings may not necessarily be about the metal in question.

grimoire: (Medieval French, "grammar") A handbook or "grammar" of magic from the Middle Ages or Renaissance periods. Grimoires make up the most significant body of medieval magical literature. Their focus is almost entirely on goetic magic — that is, the art of summoning spirits and demons to do the bidding of the magician — although a certain amount of natural magic appears in some examples as well. The most famous of the grimoires include the *Picatrix*, the *Key of Solomon*, the *Lemegeton*, the *Sworn Book of Honorius*, the *Grand Grimoire*, and the *Dragon Rouge* ("Red Dragon"); there were many others.

The magic of the grimoires is a free mix of methods from many different sources, of which Jewish, Arabic, Greek, and medieval Christian elements are the most visible. The magician was instructed to make and consecrate a variety of working tools, lay out a magical circle for protection against the spirits, and then repeat a series of prayers, conjurations, and commands to induce the desired spirit to appear. Once the spirit arrived, it could be commanded to consecrate talismans, prophesy the future, reveal the location of hidden treasure, and so on.

The popularity of the grimoires was at its height in the late Middle Ages, and began to wane with the spread of Renaissance high magic in the later sixteenth century. They have nonetheless remained in use up to the present time, and a number of more recent magical traditions have drawn heavily from one or another grimoire. Some of the magical handbooks presently used in American folk magic, such as the Sixth and Seventh Books of Moses, draw on the older Grimoire lore.

group mind: In magical parlance, the collective consciousness of a group of people whose emotions and thoughts are focused in the same direction. Mob behavior and many other quirks of social psychology, according to occult teachings, are generated by group minds that are formed at random, generally by people who have no notion of what is going on. The deliberate construction of a group mind, on the other hand, is an important part in the construction of a working magical lodge. *SEE* LODGE, MAGICAL.

Hermes Trismegistus: (Greek, "Hermes Thrice Great")
The mythical founder of Hermeticism, Hermes Trismegistus began his career as the ancient Egyptian god Djehuti or Thoth, among whose titles was "three times great." After the Greek conquest of Egypt under Alexander the Great, Thoth became identified with Hermes, the closest equivalent among the Greek gods, and his title was translated as well. Over time, with the emergence of a hybrid Greek-Egyptian culture in the Nile valley, the ancient Egyptian habit of crediting Thoth with the authorship of all books on magic carried over to Hermes, and a genre of Greek books on magic and mysticism took shape in what came to be called the Hermetic tradition. *SEE* HERMETICISM.

Few people in ancient times, and even fewer in the Middle Ages, doubted that Hermes Trismegistus had been a flesh-and-blood person who had lived at a distant time in the past and written important books of magic, astrology, alchemy, and theology. Efforts were made starting in

Roman times to provide him with a biography, and these accelerated as Pagan gods became less acceptable and human sages more so.

Even in the Hermetic writings themselves, the Hermes who appears is sometimes described as the grandson of an older Hermes, who is clearly enough the god Thoth; later on, efforts to reinterpret Hermes as a historical figure became all but universal. Thus, for example, Jewish writers commonly identified Hermes with Enoch, while Muslim scholars considered him to be the same person as the mysterious Idris who initiated Moses. Since Enoch was held to have become the mighty angel Metatron after his assumption into heaven, while Idris has nearly as exalted a status in Islamic legend and lore, both these identifications give the Thrice Great One as close to his former divine status as a monotheistic religion can provide.

By the early Middle Ages, the figure of Hermes had changed shape once again, and an entire literature of magical, astrological, and alchemical books was attached to his still-famous name. To the medieval mind, Hermes was a contemporary of Moses, an Egyptian priest, prophet, and king who had single-handedly invented alchemy, astrology, magic, and a variety of other arts. Attempts to redefine Hermes Trismegistus in historical terms have continued up to the present. In the teachings of the American Rosicrucian order AMORC, for instance, the heretic pharaoh Akhenaten is defined as the "second Hermes," despite the fact that the teachings of Akhenaten, which are well attested historically, are about as far from Hermeticism as can be imagined; *SEE* AKHENATEN.

Hermeticism: One of the core elements in the Western occult tradition, Hermeticism had its roots in the fusion of Greek philosophy and Egyptian magic that took place in Egypt after its conquest by Alexander the Great in 332 BCE. While Egyptians were slow to accept the ways of their Greek conquerors, the Greeks themselves readily took up the worship of Egyptian gods, and the political advantages of fluency and literacy in Greek were not lost on the Egyptian priesthood.

Thus, over time, a bilingual and bicultural society emerged along the banks of the Nile in which millennia old Egyptian magic and spirituality could be reformulated in the terms of Greek thought. The career of Chaeremon, an Egyptian priest of the first century CE who was also a Stoic philosopher of international fame, shows how far this process extended.

At some point within a century or so of the beginning of the Common Era, this context began to respond to the same spiritual impulse that drove the rise of Neoplatonism, Gnosticism, Manichaeism, and Christianity—a sense of entrapment in the world of ordinary experience, and a longing for a way of escape. The causes of this trend are complex and still much debated. The results were equally complex and varied widely, depending on the resources available to philosophers and mystics in different parts of the ancient world. In the Nile valley, the central resources were those of ancient Egyptian spirituality, and the result was Hermeticism.

Very little trace has survived of the original Hermetic schools and teachings. From clues in the remaining writings, scholars have guessed that the Hermetic tradition was developed and transmitted in small, informal circles of students gathered around charismatic teachers. Mystical philosophy, ceremonial magic, astrology, and alchemy were all part of the course of study, and all these were intended to lead to an experience of rebirth in which the individual soul realized its connection with the supreme, nameless divine power of the universe. Just as ancient Egyptian books of magic were all credited to Thoth, rather than to their human authors, the books produced by these circles were attributed to Hermes Trismegistus, the Greek equivalent of Thoth. *SEE* HERMES TRISMEGISTUS.

The massive cultural charisma of Egypt in the ancient world gave these books, and the Hermetic tradition itself, a reputation for deep wisdom that made them attractive to students of many other spiritual traditions. Among Platonists and Neoplatonists, though there were always those who rejected overtly magical traditions such as Hermeticism, there were equally those who embraced them as a useful resource. This latter approach became increasingly common with the rise of Christianity, as Pagan traditions that had formerly spent much time quarreling with one another sought common ground in the face of a common threat. At the hands of Iamblichus of Chalcis, who sought to create a unified Pagan spirituality as a bulwark against the Christian tide, Hermetic magic became a key element in this system.

The Christians themselves were not immune to the aura of wisdom that surrounded "Egyptian Mysteries," and a number of church fathers did their best to co-opt Hermetic writings in support of Christianity, going to the extent of forging "oracles of Hermes" that predicted the coming of Jesus. This had an unexpected effect; because Hermes Trismegistus ended up wearing the ill-fitting label of a prophet of Christ, Hermetic documents that might otherwise have been consigned to the flames were preserved and copied through the Middle Ages. A good deal of Hermeticism thus survived in Christian garb, giving rise to Christian occult traditions; *SEE* CHRISTIAN OCCULTISM.

The Arab invasions of the eighth century replaced one dogmatic religion with another in Egypt and through much of the Mediterranean world. The Muslim conquerors absorbed many of the cultural traditions of the peoples they overran, however, and a large body of Hermetic practice was taken over both by mystically minded Muslims and by Arab magicians. The Quran, the holy book of Islam, also provided a loophole for Hermeticists by including "Sabians" among the Peoples of the Book, who were to be permitted to follow their own religions unmolested by good Muslims; exactly what the term "Sabians" meant has been a subject of centuries of argument, but in the centuries after the Muslim conquests it was widely interpreted to mean Hermeticists. The Pagan town of Harran took advantage of this to preserve their own religious traditions, which were heavily mixed with Hermeticism and Neoplatonism.

Hermetic traditions of spiritual and practical magic thus became part of the broad current of Arabic magic that flowed into Europe beginning in the twelfth century CE. The more theoretical side of Hermeticism was also preserved in a handful of books. During the Middle Ages, the most important of these was the Asclepius, which survived in a Latin translation in the West. Further east, in the Byzantine Empire, a collection of Hermetic texts later known as the *Corpus Hermeticum* was preserved, although it seems to have had little circulation; *SEE* CORPUS HERMETICUM.

Several astrological books under Hermes' name were also available early on, and Arabic magical handbooks such as the *Picatrix* also contained a certain amount of Hermetic philosophy. There were also purely magical texts to be had with Hermes' name on them, such as *Liber Hermetis dc quindecim stellis (Book of IIermes on the fifteen stars)*, a handbook of talismanic magic that was widely copied throughout the Middle Ages and Renaissance. Despite the occasional suspicions of the church, a steady undercurrent of interest in Hermes and his teachings continued in educated circles throughout the medieval period. Important Platonists such as Bernardus Sylvestris (fl. twelfth century) used it as a resource, though they rarely cited it by name. *SEE* PLATONISM.

The recovery of the *Corpus Hermeticum* by the West, by way of a single Greek manuscript obtained by Cosimo dc Medici of Florence around 1460 and translated into Latin by Marsilio Ficino in 1463, transformed this undercurrent into a flood. Ficino himself, his pupil Giovanni Pico della Mirandola, and a constellation of later scholars and magicians used the Hermetic writings as the foundation for an ambitious attempt to create a new Christian occultism, drawing on magical techniques and directed toward spiritual and practical ends alike. This program probably reached its zenith in 1591, when the Croatian Hermeticist Francesco Patrizi (1529–1597) formally proposed that the philosophy of Aristotle and Thomas Aquinas should be replaced by that of Hermes as the intellectual foundation of Catholic theology. The proposal was rejected, but only after serious consideration, and the fact that it was made at all shows the degree to which Hermetic thought had permeated the intellectual life of the Renaissance.

Not long after Patrizi's proposal, however, Hermeticism suffered a major blow when Isaac Casaubon demonstrated on linguistic grounds that the treatises of the *Corpus Hermeticum* dated not from the time of Moses, but from the early centuries of the Common Era. Casaubon's work, published in 1614, marks the effective end of Renaissance Hermeticism. Afterwards, though committed Hermeticists and occultists continued to study the Hermetic writings, European culture in general threw them aside as discredited forgeries.

Until very recently, although the label "Hermetic" was much used by a variety of magical societies, the actual teachings of classical Hermeticism received little attention. The nineteenth-century occult revival saw the reprinting of the *Corpus Hermeticum* and other ancient Hermetic documents, but for the most part the Hermetic teachings were reinterpreted through the filters of Theosophy and similar occult philosophies.

That began to change in the 1960s, as a new generation of occultists encountered the scholarly writings of Dame

Frances Yates, who almost single-handedly reintroduced the Hermetic tradition into the world of modern scholarship. Yates' writings argued that Hermeticism had a massive influence on all levels of Renaissance culture, and sparked a great deal of debate and further research in academic circles. At the same time, and without those circles' knowledge, these same books became required reading for educated magicians all over the Western world, and catalyzed a variety of efforts to explore older levels of magical tradition and reclaim Western occultism's own historical roots.

horary astrology: The art of astrological divination in which a chart is cast for the moment at which a specific question is asked, and interpreted as an answer to the question. Horary astrology was once among the most popular branches of astrology, and formed the bread and butter of astrological practice before the Scientific Revolution. It fell out of popularity with the rise of psychological approaches to astrology in the nineteenth century, but has experienced a modest revival in the latter part of the twentieth century.

Horary astrology starts with a specific question and a specific moment in time. The question must be one that can be assigned to one of the twelve astrological houses; *SEE* HOUSE, ASTROLOGICAL. The chart is erected just like a birth chart, using the place and time in which the question was asked. The person asking the question, who is called the querent, is symbolized by the first house of the chart; the subject of the question is called the quesited, and is represented by whatever astrological house the question relates to. For example, a question about a marriage relates to the seventh house, and this would be the house of the quesited in a horary chart drawn up to answer the question.

In astrology, the cusp of each house falls in one of the signs of the zodiac, and each zodiacal sign is ruled by a planet. This is the key to horary interpretation. The astrologer, having identified the houses of the querent and quesited, identifies the planets whose signs are on the cusps of the two houses in question, and looks for an astrological relationship between the planets in the chart. There are various possible relationships, each with its traditional interpretation. Reading of the meanings of the relationships, or noting there are none—traditionally a negative sign—the horary astrologer can provide the answer to the question. *SEE ALSO* ASTROLOGY.

horoscope: In modern astrological terminology, a chart of the heavens at a particular moment as they relate to a specific point on the surface of the Earth. The word "horoscope" originally meant what is now called the ascendant—that is, the degree of the zodiac at the eastern horizon at the moment for which the chart is cast—and took on its present meaning in the late Middle Ages.

Until recent times, the standard format for a horoscope was square, divided into twelve triangular areas and a central square by straight lines. In the days before preprinted blanks, this form of chart was much easier to draw. Over the last two centuries, a circle divided into twelve wedges has become more common.

house, astrological: One of twelve sections of the heavens as seen from a particular place and time on Earth. The astrological houses were among the last ingredients to be added to classical astrology, and in Roman times they were still in competition with alternative divisions of the sky into four or eight sections.

There are a number of different systems of house division, based on different mathematical ways of dividing up the sky. Among the most common nowadays are the Placidus system, the Koch system, and the Equal House system. Different astrologers favor different systems, and there seems to be no basis for defining one or another as "right."

In medieval, Renaissance, and modern astrology, the twelve houses refer to twelve basic categories of things in human life, and a planet or sign in one of the houses will have its strongest influence on that part of the horoscope.

There is some variation in the aspects of life that are assigned to different houses; the list given here is from medieval sources.

First House: the querent, or the person for whom the divination is performed.

Second House: goods, material wealth, gain, business transactions, material things the querent desires, and stolen property.

Third House: brothers and sisters, the querent's neighbors and environment, short journeys, letters, advice, news and rumors.

Fourth House: father and mother, inheritances from parents, land, agriculture, buildings, construction, treasures, anything underground, ancient places and things, old age, hidden things, and the end of any matter.

Fifth House: pregnancy, children, entertainments and feasts, bodies of water, and rain.

Sixth House: servants, employees, small animals, illness, and injuries.

Seventh House: the querent's spouse or lover, love relationships, marriage, partnerships, quarrels, any unidentified person.

Eighth House: suffering, death, dangers, inheritances (other than from parents).

Ninth House: religion, philosophy, learning and education, the arts, wisdom, long journeys, divination.

Tenth House: employment, position in society, people in positions of authority, courts and judges, and the weather.

Eleventh House: friends, sources of help, good fortune, the querent's hopes and wishes.

Twelfth House: enemies, suffering, difficulties, any secret matter, imprisonment, large animals, the querent's fears.

In the case of zodiacal signs, the cusp or beginning of the sign is the important point for determining its house placement; if a sign has its cusp in one house, that sign rules that house, even if most of the sign overlaps into another house. *SEE ALSO* ASTROLOGY.

initiation: (Latin *initiatio*, "beginning") One of the most confused and complex terms in modern occult parlance, the word "initiation" was originally borrowed from fraternal lodge organizations such as Freemasonry, where it was used to refer to the ceremony by which a member was advanced to a particular grade or degree, receiving the teachings, rights, and formal title of that level of membership. In the eighteenth and nineteenth centuries, the concept of lodge degrees became fused with ideas of the process of spiritual development, and this caused the concept of initiation to take on a great deal of additional baggage. As a result, nineteenth- and early twentieth-century writings often treat initiation as something vastly mysterious, involving Hidden Masters and out-of-body experience.

All this has very little to do with the reality of initiation as actually practiced by magical lodge organizations, Wiccan covens, and other occult groups. The ceremonies of initiation worked by such groups can have powerful psychological and spiritual effects on those who pass through them, especially when amplified by the technical methods of ritual magic. Still, they are not particularly complex in terms of their basic structure and operation.

Details vary widely, but in outline, most initiations start by secluding the candidate—the person to be initiated—while a space is prepared, physically and magically, for the ceremony. The candidate is commonly blindfolded before being brought into the space, and may be walked around in circles, startled by sudden noises or physical contact, or left in silence and darkness for a period. All this serves to create a state of heightened receptivity in the candidate.

While in this state, the candidate is taken through a set of symbolic experiences that encode the teachings of the degree through sounds, words, physical contact and movement, and other stimuli. The blindfold will usually be raised at one point or another to reveal important images. At some point during this process, the candidate takes an oath or obligation, binding himself or herself to abide by the rules of the order, coven, lodge, or other group.

At some point after the oath or obligation, the candidate receives the secrets of the degree—typically a set of grips, passwords, symbolic gestures, and other identifying signs. These ground the experience of initiation in the candidate's body; when the same signs are repeated by the candidate, as they will be at every subsequent working of that degree, they function as somatic triggers that reawaken the emotional states the candidate experienced during the initiation. The ritual typically closes with one or more lectures on the teachings of the degree, which serve to "talk the candidate down" from his or her altered state, and also to communicate useful information.

This pattern of initiation is all but universal in those Western occult traditions that practice ceremonial workings, although alternative methods based on the very different Hindu or Buddhist initiation patterns have been introduced by a few groups, especially in central Europe. Many initiation rituals have been published, including those of such influential groups as Gardnerian Wicca and the Hermetic Order of the Golden Dawn. *SEE ALSO* DE-GREE; LODGE, MAGICAL.

Jachin: (Hebrew, "he has established") One of the two pillars at the door of the Temple of Solomon, an important element of Cabalistic, magical, and Masonic symbolism. The pillar Jachin stood at the right of the entrance of the temple. In symbolism, it is often shown as white, and corresponds to the active, the spiritual, and the masculine, as the pillar Boaz corresponds to the receptive or passive, the material, and the feminine. Cabalists associate Jachin with the right-hand pillar of the Tree of Life, the Pillar of Mercy. *SEE* TREE OF LIFE. In many Masonic lodges, the pillar Jachin is topped with a globe of the heavens, representing its association with the celestial world. *SEE* FREEMASONRY. *SEE ALSO* BOAZ; TEMPLE OF SOLOMON.

Jung, Carl Gustav: Swiss psychologist and occultist, 1875–1961. Among the most influential figures in modern psychology, Carl Jung was born into a family whose backgrounds defined much of his future life. His father was a

Protestant minister from a line of eminent scholars and theologians, while his mother came from a family deeply involved in occult and spiritualistic practices. He enrolled in the medical school of Basel University in 1895, and finished his studies there at the end of 1900. His dissertation, "On the Psychology and Pathology of So-Called Occult Phenomena," was based on séances he himself had conducted with members of his family, using his cousin Hélène Preiswerk as the medium.

Fresh out of medical school, he went to work at the Burghölzli Mental Hospital in Zurich, where he carried out widely acclaimed studies in word association as a diagnostic tool. He and the head of the hospital, Eugen Bleuler (1857–1939), were among the first physicians outside Vienna to take up psychoanalysis, the new and extremely controversial system of therapy then being developed by Sigmund Freud (1856–1939) in Vienna. From 1905 to 1912, Jung was among the most influential figures in the Freudian community, rising to the position of president of the International Psychoanalytic Association.

In 1912, however, Jung broke publicly with Freud, rejecting much of the older man's theories in favor of a more radical and in many ways more spiritual approach to psychotherapy. Jung argued that along with the personal unconscious, which consists of things forgotten or repressed during the individual's life, there is also a collective unconscious, which consists of archaic patterns—archetypes—that correspond to primitive human instincts, on the one hand, and the gods of Pagan religion, on the other.

Lying behind Jung's theories was a long association with the occult. His library contained many books by Theosophical mystic and scholar G. R. S. Mead (1863–1933), and after his break with Freud he became a frequent visitor and speaker at the School of Wisdom in Darmstadt, a center for occult studies founded by Baltic occultist Count Hermann Keyserling (1880–1947). Like many German occultists, Jung was particularly interested in the ancient Persian traditions of Zoroastrianism and Mithraism, and also in Gnosticism. Jung himself recorded dreams and visionary experiences in which he encountered Gnostic deities and was transformed into Aion, the lion-headed Mithraic deity. *SEE* GNOSTICISM.

In his later career, Jung became deeply interested in the traditions of alchemy, and came to believe that the alchemists had been practicing psychotherapy, using chemical reactions as a blank slate on which to project psychological transformations. He was also a practicing astrologer, having learned to erect horoscopes from his colleague and lover Antonia Wolff (1888–1953) in 1911, and played a central role in introducing the Western world to the I Ching by writing an influential foreword to Richard Wilhelm's famous 1950 translation.

Jung left the Burghölzli in 1909 to go into private practice, and moved to Küsnacht, near Zurich, where he built
a stone tower and led a busy career as therapist, teacher,
and author. He became an increasingly famous public
figure, not only in Europe but in North America as well,
where Jungian ideas took hold in the 1920s and became
extremely popular by the time of Jung's death.

Kether: (Hebrew KThR, "crown") The first and highest Sephirah of the Cabalistic Tree of Life and the highest Sephirah of the Middle Pillar. Kether is the first manifestation, the original unity from which all else unfolds, and the goal of the spiritual quest as understood by the Cabala. Its standard correspondences are as follows:

Name of God: AHIH, Eheieh (I Am).

Archangel: MITTRVN, Metatron, the Prince of Countenances.

Angelic Host: ChIVTh HQDSh, Chaioth haQodesh (Holy Living Creatures).

Astrological Correspondence: RAShITh HGLGLIM, Rashith ha-Gilgalim (Beginnings of Turnings or Primum Mobile).

Tarot Correspondence: The four Aces of the pack.

Elemental Correspondence: Air.

Magical Image: A human face looking toward the viewer's right, seen through brilliant light. Some versions make this a bearded male face, others present it as androgynous.

Additional Symbols: The point, the crown.

Additional Titles: Macroprosopus, the Greater Countenance; Amen; the Primordial Point; the Head Which Is Not; Ancient of Days.

Colors: in Atziluth—pure brilliance.
   in Briah—brilliant white.
   in Yetzirah—brilliant white.
   in Assiah—white, flecked with gold.

Correspondence in the Microcosm: Yechidah, the spiritual essence of the self.

Correspondence in the Body: Above the crown of the head.

Grade of Initiation: 10=1, Ipsissimus.

Qlippoth: ThAVMIAL, Thaumiel, the Divided Ones.

The text of the Thirty-two Paths of Wisdom associated with Kether runs, "The First Path is called the Admirable or Hidden Intelligence, for it is the Light giving the power of comprehension of that First Principle which has no beginning; and it is the Primal Glory, for no created being can attain to its essence." *SEE ALSO* CABALA; TREE OF LIFE.

Kybalion, The: Perhaps the most influential work to come out of the American occult scene in the twentieth century, *The Kybalion* was written by American occultists William Walker Atkinson (also known by his pen name Yogi Ramacharaka), Paul Foster Case, and Michael Witty, then head of the Alpha et Omega magical lodges in North America. Published anonymously in 1912 as the work of "Three Initiates," it quickly became standard reading in most American occult circles and remains popular in the more traditionally oriented magical groups to this day.

The Kybalion is organized as a commentary on a supposedly ancient collection of Hermetic axioms handed down from master to pupil for centuries; this collection is also (and confusingly) called *The Kybalion*. As usual in matters of this sort, no trace of a collection of this name appears in the very well-documented history of Hermeticism before 1912; *SEE* HERMETICISM. The commentary focuses on a set of seven "Hermetic Principles," as follows:

The Principle of Mentalism, which holds that all phenomena are ultimately mental, and that physical matter is a product of the universal Mind;

the Principle of Correspondence, which holds that the same principles and patterns hold true on every level of existence;

the Principle of Vibration, which holds that all the different levels of existence are simply different rates of vibration of one primary, mental substance;

the Principle of Polarity, which holds that all things contain two opposing aspects, and all opposites are aspects of some unity;

the Principle of Rhythm, which holds that all things have a rhythm between their two opposing aspects, which gives rise to an infinite number of rhythmic cycles of action and reaction;

the Principle of Cause and Effect, which holds that all things are the effect of some cause and the cause of some effect, and that nothing happens by chance;

and the Principle of Gender, which holds that there are masculine and feminine principles in everything and on all planes, and that all creation takes place through contact between these two.

While *The Kybalion* almost certainly does not have the ancient origins claimed for it, these seven principles very adequately sum up the basic concepts of modern Hermetic philosophy, and the book has certainly earned its reputation among occultists as one of the fundamental texts of a modern magical education.

Lemegeton, the: Among the most famous of the medieval grimoires, the *Lemegeton* consists of five books—the *Goetia*, the *Theurgia Goetia*, the *Art Pauline*, the *Art Almadel*, and the *Artem Novem*—each dedicated to a different branch of the art of evoking spirits. The meaning of the word "Lemegeton" remains unknown, and the collection is also known as the *Lesser Key of Solomon*; SEE SOLOMON.

The first book, the *Goetia*, is by far the most famous, and has been reprinted numerous times on its own. It consists of a list of seventy-two demons, along with their seals, their special powers, and full ritual instructions for summoning and commanding them.

The *Goetia* has retained its popularity as a source for evocations into modern times, and is still commonly used by a range of magical practitioners. Its list of spirits and their seals are included in the *Bok of the Art Magical*, the first version of Gerald Gardner's Book of Shadows. The same collection of spirits and seals has also been made the basis for a divination system and a fantasy wargame.

The remaining portions offer additional rituals and smaller collections of spirits who can be summoned and commanded for a variety of special purposes. The *Theurgia Goetia* deals with aerial spirits, some good and some evil; the *Art Pauline* discusses the spirits governing the planetary hours, degrees of the zodiac, and planets; the *Art Almadel* concerns a set of twenty spirits associated with the seasons, who can be summoned for certain specified purposes; and the *Artem Novemor*, "New Art," consists of instructions for summoning good spirits through theurgic means. Much less attention has been paid to these latter sections in recent times. *SEE ALSO* GRIMOIRE.

lamp: In several traditions of ceremonial magic, a working tool representing the presence of spirit or the divine in the temple. The magical lamp is similar to, and probably inspired by, the Presence lamp kept burning in some Christian denominations as a symbol of the presence of God.

lodge, magical: The standard social form for Western occultism during most of the modern period, the magical lodge is an odd hybrid derived mostly from contemporary fraternal lodge systems. Occult writers during the Golden

Age of magical lodges (roughly 1780–1950) claimed that their lodges, and the lodge system as a whole, dated to ancient times and had been preserved intact for thousands of years. This is inaccurate. The magical lodge system was borrowed almost entirely from fraternal lodge traditions such as Freemasonry, taking not only its basic structure but most of its details from this source. SEE FREE-MASONRY.

The earliest magical lodges took shape on the fringes of French and German Freemasonry around the middle of the eighteenth century. While there had been occult secret societies of various kinds before that time, of course, the standard toolkit of the magical lodge—ritual initiations, an ascending ladder of degrees, passwords, secret handshakes, and the like—were an eighteenth-century addition. This set of fraternal lodge methods was combined with older occult traditions by figures such as Martinez de Pasqually and Karl Gotthelf von Hund, founders respectively of the Élus Coens and the Strict Observance, two important early magical lodge organizations.

Pasqually and von Hund, like many later magical lodge designers, also drew heavily on legends about various older secret societies such as the Rosicrucians and the Knights Templar. Early magical lodges also drew a surprising amount of their imagery and internal mythology from a far less reputable source—the vast structure of conspiracy theories that arose in Europe in the aftermath of the French Revolution, and blossomed into hysteria in the wake of the popular insurrections across Europe in the 1820s and 1840s. Whatever the political risks of borrowing such imagery, it was colorful, and it promoted the idea that magical orders were vast, powerful, and well organized—a claim that was useful for recruitment purposes. Thus staples of conspiracy literature such as *aqua toffana* entered into many of the texts of the nineteenth-century magical revival.

The result was the rise of a mythology of magical lodges, which can be seen in its full flower in fictional works such as Dion Fortune's "Doctor Taverner" short stories. According to the mythology, magical lodges had been in continuous existence since ancient Egyptian times, if not since Atlantis itself; they had worldwide connections, and exercised subtle but powerful influence over everything that happened in the world; they were led by mysterious, secluded adepts with superhuman abilities; and they guarded vast quantities of secret teachings that had never been revealed to outsiders, and which conferred miraculous powers over the physical world.

In point of actual fact, none of this was true. The magical lodges of the eighteenth, nineteenth, and early twentieth centuries were recent creations cobbled together from scraps of older lore, and few of them lasted beyond the lifespans of their original founders. Few had more than a dozen individual lodges, and fewer still had more than a hundred members. With a very small handful of exceptions—cases in which a member of one or another order happened to rise to an important political office—they had no noticeable political influence. Their leaders, like the rank-and-file members, were ordinary human beings whose interest in occultism did not keep them from having to earn a living or deal with the ordinary issues of everyday life. The teachings of the magical lodges, finally, were derived either from publicly available sources or from the personal research of the orders' founders and leading members, and constantly trickled out into print.

There have been three main waves of magical lodges over the years, each with its own characteristics. The first, which dates from the late eighteenth century, was essentially an offshoot of Freemasonry and drew nearly all its rituals and methods from that source. The lodges of this first wave tended to restrict membership to Master Masons, and were thus open to men only. Their occult teachings were generally very specialized—particular methods of alchemy, ritual magic, or other branches of occult practice were taught, but no attempt was made to present a complete study course in occultism. The initiations were the central feature of these lodges; the teachings were simply one of the benefits to be gained by being initiated. The Orden des Gold- und Rosenkreuz (Order of the Golden and Rosy Cross), a German order of the late eighteenth century, is a typical and well-documented example of this type.

The second wave took shape in the second half of the nineteenth century, and was influenced both by the first wave and by the great European occult revival of the time. Lodges of the second wave varied widely in how much material they drew from Masonry; many did not require Masonic affiliation, and several opened their doors to women. Orders of this second wave put approximately equal stress on their initiations and their teachings. In many cases, the teachings themselves were expanded into full-scale study courses in occult theory and practice. The Hermetic Order of the Golden Dawn is far and away the best known of this type.

The third wave began in the last years of the nineteenth century and reached full flood between the two world wars. Magical lodges of this third type generally had little if anything to do with Freemasonry or other fraternal orders, and their teachings were increasingly central to their work. Most of them functioned mainly as correspondence schools, and offered initiation and lodge activity as one of the benefits to be gained by advancing through the different lessons of the course. Examples of the type include such well-known modern orders as AMORC and BOTA.

Like the fraternal lodges from which they borrowed so much, most magical lodges went into a steep decline in the second half of the twentieth century. The reasons for this are complex and still not well understood, but the somewhat stuffy ritual and hierarchical structures of many magical lodge organizations did not appeal to the young, counterculture-influenced people who flocked into occultism in the wake of the Sixties. Some magical lodges still remain active at the present time, and others have been revived on the basis of written materials. While they are unlikely to dominate the magical field they way they once did, magical lodges will probably be a noticeable element in the occult scene for some time to come.

magic: Perhaps the most complex concept in Western occultism, magic has been, defined and understood in a dizzying variety of ways over the centuries. At present, there is no single meaning generally accepted, even within the occult community, and the definitions used by occultists differ immensely from those proposed by academics and those held by the man or woman in the street. A history of these different definitions is, to a large extent, a history of magic itself.

Originally, the word—in Greek, *mageia*; in Latin, *magia*—meant the knowledge or art of the *magoi* or *magi*, a hereditary caste of Persian holy men. The Greek historian Herodotus ascribes to the magoi the responsibility for sacrifices, funeral ceremonies, and divination at the Persian royal court, and Xenophon describes them as experts in all things concerning the gods. As a borrowed term in Greek and Roman society, it had something of the same cachet that the word "swami" had in twentieth-century America—

suggesting something strange, mystical, possibly impressive, possibly suspect.

The word "magus" had several competitors in ancient times, each of which came to refer to a particular class of what we would now label "magicians." The Greek word *goes* originally referred to a type of professional mourner in archaic funeral rites, and gradually shifted meanings over time to refer to the lowest class of magical practitioner, a mediumistic communicator with the dead; it could also mean "charlatan." On a much higher level was the *theios aner* or "divine man," a person who had gained magical powers by asceticism and devotion to the gods. Apollonius of Tyana is among the most widely known examples of the type, and Jesus of Nazareth may have been another. The polemics over magic in ancient times made for a situation in which any or all of these labels might be applied to the same person; a given magician might well be called a *theios aner* by his clients and supporters, a *goes* by his enemies, and a *magos* by the population at large. By the beginning of the Common Era, the words "magus" and "magic" had lost most of their Persian connotations, and were used for most of the same practices that are still called "magical" today—that is, ritual workings and special preparations of substances meant to affect the universe by methods that don't make sense in the framework of modern scientific thought.

This widening of the concept of magic caused a certain degree of difficulty, because prohibitions of magic were on the lawbooks of Rome long before Christianity rose to dominance. The Roman state had a long-term paranoia about private spiritual activities, which burst out in such atrocities as the execution of thousands of Diony sian initiates in 186 BCE and the persecution of Christians at various times in the first, second, and third centuries of the Common Era; all forms of magic potentially fell under the same draconian laws. Traditional practices in agriculture, medicine, and many crafts found themselves reclassified as magic, and hasty exemptions had to be granted in some cases to keep these from falling under the severe legal penalties for magical practice. This widened definition of magic went through several shifts as Christianity rose to dominance in the Roman world, the Roman state itself collapsed, and the new societies of medieval Europe took shape. Paradoxically, the rise of Christianity actually decreased the persecution of magic for some centuries, as the early church defined "magic" as any form of occult practice that called upon non-Christian deities or powers. Identical rituals invoking the Trinity or the saints were explicitly exempted, and so a huge body of Christian magical practice grew up, tacitly permitted (and on occasion, actively supported) by church officials and theologians. *SEE* CHRISTIAN OCCULTISM.

The later Middle Ages, however, saw a sharp upswing in the persecution of magic. Partly this was a function of the severe stress undergone by the medieval world in the fourteenth century, the age of the Black Death of 1347–1352 and the social convulsions that followed it. Much of the renewed assault on magic, though, was actually due to the revival of studies of ancient Roman law in the universities. The old Roman classification of magic was widely discussed, and the idea that magic was magic no matter what entities were invoked became common among European intellectuals and lawyers. This shift played a significant part in launching the age of witch hunting that modern Pagans call the Burning Times.

The same revival of classical learning that helped start the Burning Times also, paradoxically enough, set in motion a very different redefinition of magic. The recovery of ancient mystical and magical texts from Greece and Rome led to the burgeoning of Renaissance Hermeticism, which saw magical practice as a religious act, a way of participation in the divine. *SEE* HERMETICISM. In the hands of Christian Hermeticists such as Marsilio Ficino (1433–1499) and Giovanni Pico della Mirandola (1463–1494), Renaissance Hermeticism became a more literate and philosophically sophisticated version of the magical Christianity of the early Middle Ages. In the hands of more radical figures such as Giordano Bruno (1548–1600), it became an independent religion in its own right, one that claimed to be older and wiser than Christianity. It was for making such claims that Bruno was burned at the stake. Both the Christian and the non-Christian view of magic as a religious rite remained common in the occult community itself until the rise of new definitions of magic in the nineteenth and twentieth centuries.

The next great shift in opinions about magic started out with the Protestant Reformation of the sixteenth century, and was the product of a radical redefinition of religion that took root in the arguments between Protestant and Catholic factions in the years that followed. Protestant polemicists in England, seeking a way to denounce Catholic ritualism, argued that religion consists entirely of turning toward the divine in hope and trust, and waiting passively for a response. Any action that seeks to influence, direct, or command spiritual powers, they argued, was magic, not religion. This line of argument was moderately effective as a way of attacking Catholicism, but its greatest impact was in another field. During the eighteenth and nineteenth century, a series of Protestant theologians and philosophers built an entire theory of religion on this basis, which went on to become standard throughout the English-speaking and German-speaking countries of the world. From there it passed into comparative religion and anthropology, not least because it allowed the religions of non-European peoples to be dismissed as magic, not religion. To this day, a noticeable percentage of books written about magic by academics quote this same distinction between magic and religion as though it were a universal truth. In fact, with the exception of a few forms of Protestant Christianity, every religion in the world deals with spiritual powers by a combination of approaches, some more passive, some less so.

The multiple impacts of the Reformation and the Scientific Revolution thus brought about vast shifts in the definitions of magic used in the Western world. While clergymen denounced magic as an affront to the omnipotence of the Christian god, and scientists scratched their heads wondering why people could believe something that so obviously couldn't be true, magical practitioners themselves gradually evolved definitions of their own. This project was launched primarily by the work of French magus Eliphas Lévi (1810–1875), whose synthesis and redefinition of traditional occultism kick-started the modern magical revival. Lévi defined magic as the art of manipulating the Astral Light, the mysterious substance-energy that in his view lay behind all magical activities. Later writers, drawing on Lévi's theory of the magical will, expanded the definition considerably. The English magus and self-proclaimed Antichrist Aleister Crowley (1875–1947) proclaimed that magic—or as he spelled it, "magick"—is "the science and art of causing change in conformity with will." This definition, of course, would include anything from evoking the fiends of Hell to buttering a slice of bread—a point that Crowley intended as part of an effort to break down the conceptual barriers between occultism and other forms of human action. *SEE* CROWLEY, ALEISTER. Crowley was also among the first major figures in the occult world to conceptualize magic as a discipline of spiritual transformation, along the lines of yoga or other Asian traditions of practice. English occultist Dion Fortune (1890–1946) provided a common phrasing for this concept by describing magic as "the yoga of the West." Both Fortune and Crowley were strongly influenced by the new psychology being developed in their time by Sigmund Freud (1856–1939) and Carl Jung (1875–1961), and this gave a strong impetus to their redefinition of magic as an essentially internal practice of self-development. *SEE* JUNG, CARL GUSTAV. The same was true of another highly influential figure of the same period, Israel Regardie (1907–1985), who studied the work of Freud and Jung and combined these with the concepts of Freud's oddest disciple, Wilhelm Reich (1897–1957).

In the last half of the twentieth century, a number of magical theorists came to define magic in purely psychological terms, as a method of ritual psychodrama with no effects outside the psyches of the participants. This definition found few takers in the occult community as a whole. More popular was the proposal of American mage and Druid P. E. I. Bonewits (1949–), who borrowed concepts from parapsychology to propose that magic was a set of psychological tools for making use of psychic powers such as telepathy and telekinesis.

In the light of all these competing definitions of magic, it may be foolhardy to risk another. Still, the one thing that can be said for certain about magic is that it is what magicians do. Magic, in other words, is a social category, defined by the fact that it is practiced by a particular set of subcultures—many of which have existed, in one form or another, for at least two and a half millennia in the Western world. The Pythagoreans and Orphics of classical Greece, the Gnostic and Hermetic movements of the Roman world, the occult circles of the Arab Near East, the shadowy magical and alchemical underworld of medieval Europe, the esoteric schools of Renaissance Hermeticism, the secret societies of the early modern period, the occult lodges of the eighteenth and nineteenth centuries, and the magical societies and Pagan covens of the present day all represent a single broad social phenomenon—the magical underground—distinct and coherent enough to be discussed and explored in its own terms.

As the above suggests, magic is also a historical category. Modern Western magic consists of coherent bodies of theory and practice that can be traced back some two and a half millennia through history to the occult traditions of the ancient Greek world. The term "magic" itself, as shown above, originally evolved in that ancient setting, and has remained attached to the traditions in question ever since. It thus makes sense to use the term for the traditions as such, rather than for some proposed universal category that happens to include them.

Magic, in this view, is not an abstract category of human activity, to be found in all places and times. It is a specific set of traditions found in Western cultures, and recently exported elsewhere in the world. It is directed toward shaping the world of human experience through contact with nonphysical powers, but it does so in its own distinctive and historically conditioned ways. Ways of doing the same thing that evolved in other cultural and historical settings, from this viewpoint, should not be called "magic"—any more than it would make sense for Chinese or Haitian scholars to refer to Western magical traditions as "European Taoism" or "European Voodoo."

magic square: A set of whole numbers, starting with one, arranged so that when vertical, horizontal, or diagonal lines of numbers are added together, the total is always the same. A set of seven magic squares has been traditionally assigned to the seven planets since ancient times, and are much used in talismanic magic.

By the process of gematria, the letters of a word in Hebrew or other ancient alphabets can be converted into numbers. The name of any spirit connected to a planet, turned into a sequence of numbers, can be traced out on the magic square of that planet by a connect-the-dots process, resulting in a linear design called a sigil. In ceremonial magic, the sigil of a spirit is used to summon, command, or banish the spirit. *SEE* GEMATRIA.

Magic squares made of letters rather than numbers are also found in occult tradition—though this concept only makes sense in cultures that distinguish between the two; *SEE* ARITHMANCY. The so-called "Sator-Rotas" square, formed of the Latin sentence *sator arepo tenet opera rotas*, is perhaps the most famous of these. *SEE* ARITHMOLOGY; CABALA.

Masons: *SEE* FREEMASONRY

monad: (Greek, "unit") In a variety of philosophies, some of them occult, a term for the central spiritual spark at the core of each living being. The term entered philosophical use by way of the work of the German polymath Gottfried Wilhelm Leibnitz (1646–1716), who held that monads—unconscious in the "inanimate" world, half-conscious in plants and animals, and fully conscious in humanity—were the fundamental building blocks of the entire cosmos. It was adopted by a number of mystical movements, mostly German, in the eighteenth and nineteenth centuries as a convenient term that lacked a specific anchor in existing theologies. From there it seems to have passed to Theosophy, which made much use of it. Equivalent concepts in other Western esoteric systems include the *yechidahor*, "Only One," of Cabalistic theory, and the *synteresis*, or divine spark, discussed by Plotinus and other Platonist thinkers. *SEE* CABALA; PLATONISM.

moon: One of the seven traditional astrological planets, the moon in the birth chart represents the emotional and instinctive side of the self. In astrological terms the moon rules the sign Cancer, is exalted in Taurus, is in her detriment in Capricorn, and in her fall in Scorpio. *SEE* ASTROLOGY. In alchemy, the moon is a common symbol for silver, and also represents the *albedo* or white phase of the Great Work.

motto, magical: In many contemporary magical systems, a name taken by a magician, either at the time of his or her first initiation or at some later point. Originally the magical motto was simply an alias, used to conceal one's identity at a time when being publicly engaged in magical practice was problematic. By the late nineteenth century, however, when the magical motto in its present form emerged, the motto had developed the secondary purpose of expressing the magician's central purpose or spiritual orientation.

Magical mottoes are typically in Latin, Greek, Hebrew, or Enochian, and may consist of anything from one word to an entire sentence. Very often, a magician will be referred to by the initials of his or her magical motto—thus, *Soror* (Sister) *D. N. F.* rather than *Deo Non Fortuna* (Latin for "By God, not by chance"; the motto of English occultist Violet Firth and the source of her pen name, Dion Fortune). The magical mottoes of other famous magicians may give some idea of the options. Aleister Crowley's motto was *Perdurabo* (Latin, "I will endure to the end"); Allan Bennet's was *Iehi Aour* (Hebrew, "Let there be light"); William Butler Yeats' was *Deus Est Demon Inversus* (Latin, "God is the Devil Inverted," and its initials spell out the Latin word *Dedi*, "I have given").

The custom of taking magical mottoes may have influenced the modern Neopagan custom of taking Craft names. *SEE* LODGE, MAGICAL.

Mysteries, the: Among the most famous aspects of ancient Greek and Roman religion, the Mysteries were traditional initiation rituals, many of them handed down from much earlier times. There were a variety of Mysteries available in the Greek world, and some students of mystical lore in ancient times made a habit of being initiated into as many of them as possible.

The most famous of all the Mysteries were the Eleusinian Mysteries, which were enacted once each year in the small town of Eleusis, not far from Athens. They were associated with the myth of Demeter's search for her daughter Persephone. More widespread were the Bacchic Mysteries, which centered on the myths of Dionysus; at their height, during the heyday of the Roman Empire, there were Bacchic congregations throughout the Empire, even in relative backwaters such as Britain. Other mysteries that had a wide popularity in classical times include those of Cybele, the Magna Mater or Great Mother, which spread from what is now Turkey; those of Isis, born of the fusion of Greek and Egyptian religion in the years after Alexander the Great's conquest of Egypt; and those of Mithras, which were unusual in only being open to men.

The initiation rites of the Mysteries were secret, and only scattered references and visual images survive to allow modern scholars to guess at what was involved. In the early stages of the ceremony, there were various ceremonies, some for purification and some for symbolic purposes; for example, initiates of the Eleusinian Mysteries bathed in the sea and sacrificed pigs to purify themselves, and they

traveled on foot from Athens to Eleusis along a route, the
Sacred Way, with several stops to commemorate various
events in the myth of Demeter and Persephone. There
seem to have been tests and terrifying sights, and then the
revelation of the core secret of the Mystery—something
that was seen, according to the accounts. In the Bacchic
Mysteries, for example, what was seen was a huge phallus
in a winnowing basket. What that meant, and what signifi-
cance it had to those who had passed through the initiation
ceremony, we can only guess.

Most of the Mysteries involved only a single stage
of initiation. The Eleusinian Mysteries were different in
having two phases: the *Myesisor*, or Lesser Mysteries, and
the *Teletai*, or Greater Mysteries. The Mithraic Mysteries
were a good deal more complex; they had seven degrees
of initiation, each associated with one of the seven planets known to the ancient world. The Mysteries were an
important feature of Pagan religion in the ancient world
and, like most of the other aspects of classical Paganism, they apparently went out of existence as Christianity took control of the Roman world and Pagan spiritual
practices were outlawed. Certain elements of the Mysteries were preserved in magical circles, as attested by the
Graeco-Egyptian magical papyri. Important elements of
the Greek terminology used in the papyri is borrowed

directly from the Mysteries, and there are entire rituals—for example, the so-called "Mithras Liturgy"—that seem to have been borrowed directly from Mystery rites. Since many of the more philosophical Greek and Roman magicians also sought initiation into the Mysteries, such borrowings were certainly possible, and they may have allowed some fragments of Mystery practice to pass into later magical traditions. Attempts to show specific borrowings from the Mysteries in later occultism, though, have been problematic at best so far.

Very little attention appears to have been paid to the Mysteries during the Middle Ages and the Renaissance, but the public emergence of Freemasonry in the early eighteenth century made rituals of initiation a subject of greater interest. This interest showed itself in several ways. First, attempts were made to claim (on essentially no evidence) that Freemasonry or some other fraternal order was the lineal descendant of a particular Mystery tradition or, as often as not, of the Mysteries as a whole. Second, new lodge rituals were constructed based on the scraps of surviving information about the Mysteries, a project that may have reached its zenith with the invention of the Seventh Degree of the Patrons of Husbandry, a full-scale Victorian attempt at reenacting the Eleusinian Mysteries. Third, the Mysteries were interpreted by reading back the habits and traditions of eighteenth- and nineteenth-century fraternal lodges into ancient Greece and Rome. All three of these had important effects on the development of the mythic history of occultism as it developed in the modern period; *SEE* OCCULT HISTORY.

natural magic: One of the two great divisions of Western magical practice, the other being ritual or ceremonial magic; *SEE* CEREMONIAL MAGIC. Natural magic deals with the magical powers of physical substances—herbs, stones, resins, metals, perfumes, and the like. It has generally been much less controversial than ritual magic, and has been practiced openly even at times when even a rumor of involvement in ritual magic was enough to cause imprisonment and death.

The principle governing natural magic in the Western occult tradition is the great Hermetic axiom "As above, so below." Every object in the material world, according to this dictum, is a reflection of astrological and spiritual powers. By making use of these material reflections, the natural magician concentrates or disperses particular powers of the higher levels of being; thus a stone or an herb associated with the sun is infused with the magical energies of the sun, and wearing that stone or hanging that herb on the wall brings those energies into play in a particular situation.

The philosophy and practice of natural magic are both closely associated with astrology and humoral medicine. *SEE* ASTROLOGY; MAGIC.

New Age movement: Among the most recent offshoots of the Western occult traditions, the New Age movement emerged in Britain in the 1970s among a loose network of people interested in alternative lifestyles and spiritualities. Many members of this network had been involved in "contactee" organizations—groups of people associated with the UFO phenomenon, who claimed to be in contact with extraterrestrial higher intelligences—during the 1950s and 1960s. The contactee movement during those years had been awash with apocalyptic prophecies of a New Age about to dawn, heralded by vast planetary catastrophes.

During the 1970s, a new interpretation of this idea evolved within the British network just mentioned. This idea was the suggestion that instead of waiting hopefully for the New Age to dawn, it would be more useful to live as though it had already arrived. People in the network set out to enact the New Age in daily life, and thereby help create it by inspiring others and showing that alternatives to the status quo were available. From the original circles where it was first proposed, the idea and a growing body of associated practices spread to wider alternative circles, first in Britain, then in America; by the middle of the 1980s it was functioning on a global scale.

As a movement based on opposition to existing social, cultural, and spiritual ideas, rather than on any specific doctrine of its own, the New Age has defined itself by what it is not, rather than by what it is. The resulting movement is less a single phenomenon than a grab-bag of miscellaneous beliefs united mostly by the fact that they have been more or less rejected by the scientific and cultural mainstream. Thus UFOs, channeling, alternative health-care methods, shamanism, reincarnation, Goddess worship, lost civilizations, kundalini yoga, earth myster ies, transpersonal psychology, perpetual motion schemes, the Gaia hypothesis, conspiracy theories, pyramidology, and many other equally diverse topics are all grist for the New Age mill.

This diversity makes it difficult to point to any particular set of beliefs or activities as central to the New Age movement. Still, the movement's status as a reaction against the cultural status quo provides it with a certain unity. It also serves as a connection with its historical roots.

One of the most interesting things about the New Age, in fact, is just how little of it is new. Most of the elements of the modern New Age movement were just as central to the alternative scene in Britain and America a century ago, when channelers were still called mediums, believers in ancient Goddess-worshipping matriarchies were reading Jane Harrison rather than Marija Gimbutas, physical culture and Swedish massage filled the roles of Feldenkrais training and shiatsu, and conspiracy theorists discussed czarist Russia's sinister plans rather than those of the equally sinister New World Order. It may be symptomatic that one of the most popular alternative periodicals in Britain in 1900 was titled *The New Age*.

One particular source for current New Age ideas deserves particular mention. The complicated cosmology developed by the Theosophical Society in the late nineteenth and early twentieth centuries, largely based on Helena Petrovna Blavatsky's monumental *The Secret Doctrine* (1888), includes the great majority of the ideas now central to the New Age movement, and also embodies the same across-the-board rejection of conventional ideas of science and spirituality. The entire New Age movement has been characterized as "Theosophy plus therapy," and while this is an oversimplification—there are a number of important New Age elements, such as channeling, which fall into neither of these categories—the label has a substantial element of truth to it.

The relation between the Western occult traditions and the New Age movement is a contentious issue, in large part because many present-day occultists and Pagans respond with horror to the suggestion that their traditions have anything to do with the New Age scene. Once again, though, the same relationship between a core of serious teachings on the one hand, and a much broader but much shallower penumbra of popularizations on the other, has been a factor in the history of occultism for a very long time. Alchemists in the Middle Ages wrote about the hordes of "puffers," inept would-be alchemists interested only in making gold, who were bringing the alchemical art into disrepute. Centuries later, occultists of the Victorian period shook their heads at the excesses and follies of the mesmerist and Spiritualist movements, both of which drew heavily from occult traditions.

The New Age movement is simply the most recent example of the same process. For all its awkward features, it has played an important role in recent decades in providing audiences and support to worthwhile systems of alternative medicine and spiritual practice, and in spreading occult perspectives out into Western culture as a whole.

New Thought: A spiritual movement, founded in America in the middle of the nineteenth century but presently active in many countries, which places the highest priority on the power of human thought. According to New Thought, illness and suffering are the product of negative thought patterns, and can be banished by replacing these thought patterns with other, positive ones.

The New Thought movement evolved from nineteenth-century American offshoots of Mesmerism, especially as formulated by P. P. Quimby and Mary Baker Eddy. Its roots also include the Transcendentalist movement in early nineteenth-century New England. A movement rather than an organization, New Thought spread primarily through books and lecturers and encompassed a diversity of approaches, some borrowed from occult traditions and others derived from psychology, Christianity, and other ideologies of personal growth. At certain times—for example, in the middle decades of the twentieth century— there has been a fair overlap between New Thought circles and practitioners of occult traditions, while at other times the two have appealed to different audiences and have found few points of contact.

Many New Thought ideas have been taken up in the more recent New Age movement.

Newton, Isaac: English scientist and alchemist, 1642–1727. Born to a poor family in a small Lancashire village, Newton was fascinated with mathematics and alchemy from an early age. He attended the village school, won entry into the Grantham grammar school, and in 1660 began studies at Cambridge University, where he studied mathematics and alchemy. His mathematical studies led, before his graduation in 1666, to his discovery of the binomial theorem, the invention of calculus, and other major achievements. His success in alchemy was equally marked, reaching the stage of the "peacock's tail" in the Great Work.

In 1667 he became a fellow of Trinity College, Cambridge, and pursued studies in gravitation, optics, alchemy, and biblical chronology. Like most alchemists, he was secretive about his discoveries, and most of his major publications came in the last decades of his life. His work on gravitation and cosmology, the *Principia Mathematica*, was published in 1687; his work on optics did not see print until 1704, and his work on biblical chronology and prophecy was published in two volumes after his death in 1728 and 1733. His work on alchemy remained unpublished until the late twentieth century.

Newton's alchemical activities became an embarrassment in the eighteenth century and afterwards, since alchemy—like the rest of the Western occult traditions—was dismissed as nonsense after the triumph of scientific rationalism in the early eighteenth century, and Newton himself was held up as a secular patron saint of the new scientific ideology. Thus very little attention has been paid to his long and systematic alchemical researches until quite recently, and many biographers of Newton still downplay a main interest of his life.

Notory Art: (Latin *Ars Notoria*, "Notory Art"). A nearly forgotten branch of medieval and Renaissance magic, the Notory Art or ars notoria was used to learn different branches of knowledge without the time and difficulty of studying them in the usual way. There were several different manuals of the Notory Art in circulation. In most of them, the practitioner would stare fixedly at a complicated diagram while reciting a magical conjuration. While it seems unlikely that this procedure would have suddenly filled the practitioner's head with information about a previously unknown subject, the Notory Art may well have been able to produce an artificial version of inborn talent, or the sort of intuitive understanding that makes it possible for large amounts of data to be learned and mastered in a short time. Many of the textbooks of the Notory Art were ascribed to King Solomon, the supreme magician of medieval legend, who supposedly received the entire art directly from God. *SEE* SOLOMON. Despite this, or possibly because of it, church authorities considered the Notory Art to be among the most reprehensible forms of magic, and condemned it repeatedly. Very few books on the subject have survived.

occult history: Alternative versions of history presented by occultists as the "real" history of the occult tradition or the world as a whole. While extremely common for the last century and a half, these versions are a relatively recent addition to Western occultism. Through ancient times, the Middle Ages, and the Renaissance, there seems to be no evidence that students of the occult in the Western world had opinions about history noticeably different from those of the ordinary people or the scholarly historians of their societies.

Occult history seems to have started to emerge after 1614, when Isaac Casaubon published evidence that dated the *Corpus Hermeticum* to sometime after the birth of Christ. Up to that time, students of the Hermetic writings (along with everybody else) had believed them to be authentic Egyptian teachings dating back to the time of Moses, if not before. *SEE* CORPUS HERMETICUM; HERMETICISM. Casaubon's publication was part of the widespread attack on Renaissance magical philosophy that ended the Renaissance and helped usher in the Scientific Revolution. Many occultists of the time, recognizing the political dimension of the attack, rejected Casaubon's conclusions and insisted that the *Corpus Hermeticum* was ancient Egyptian wisdom, no matter what orthodox historians said.

The rest of the seventeenth century saw little more in the way of occult history. The eighteenth century, on the other hand, marked the public emergence of Freemasonry, which sparked a historical industry that hasn't quit yet. Though all the evidence suggests that Freemasonry started out as exactly what it originally claimed to be—a trade union of stonemasons with a set of medieval guild rituals—members from the gentry and aristocracy found so working-class an origin embarrassing, and went to work trying to find something more romantic. Some of the results—the supposed connection between the Freemasons and the Knights Templar, for example, or the idea that Masonry can be traced back to ancient Egypt—are still in circulation to this day, despite an impressive lack of evidence to support them. *SEE* FREEMASONRY.

Along these same lines, the founders and promoters of other lodge organizations—many inspired by Freemasonry, some with independent origins—went to work all through the eighteenth and nineteenth centuries, producing impressive pedigrees for their own traditions. By the mid-nineteenth century, it was a poor excuse for a lodge, whether occult or fraternal, that couldn't claim to trace its origins back to ancient Egypt, Moses, the original Druids, or some equally romantic source. All these claims were elaborated and combined in various ways, giving rise to a view of history in which occult lodges were seen as the one enduring factor in the swirling tides of historical change.

The French Revolution at the end of the eighteenth century sent these speculations spinning off in new directions. Several conservative writers, unable to believe that the French people could have actually wanted to overthrow one of the most corrupt and ineffective monarchies in Europe, insisted that the revolution must have been the product of a vast and sinister conspiracy against monarchy and Christianity. The Bavarian Illuminati, a short-lived and unsuccessful secret society in Germany, was for some reason chosen by the Abbé Barruel—the first major figure in modern conspiracy theory—to play the villain of the piece. While most of the resulting furor took place outside the occult traditions of the West, elements of conspiracy theory have spilled back into occultism at intervals and provided raw materials for fabricators of occult history.

The nineteenth century saw occult history swell in other ways, as a variety of figures on the fringes of Victorian culture challenged accepted ideas. Some of them, such as Charles Darwin, were accepted by the educated establishment and brought about sweeping revisions in the way Western cultures looked at the world. Others remained on the fringes, and contributed to a growing collection of alternative viewpoints that were rejected by professional scholars and scientists but developed a following outside the official institutions of learning. One figure that made a massive contribution to occult history in this way was Ignatius Donnelly (1831–1901), a Minnesota congressman turned alternative historian who brought Plato's account of Atlantis out of relative obscurity and argued that the lost continent had actually existed. His 1882 book *Atlantis, or the Antediluvian World* relied on Victorian scientific hypotheses that were discarded during his lifetime, but its basic ideas have been copied endlessly since it first came out. His second great book, *Ragnarok, or the Age of Fire and Gravel* (1882), proposed that the Earth had collided with a comet in prehistoric times—another idea that has found an enthusiastic following in more recent versions of occult history.

The dominant figure in nineteenth-century occult history, though, was Helena Petrovna Blavatsky (1831–1891), the founder of the Theosophical Society. Blavatsky's influential writings and lectures had as a central theme the complete inadequacy of the Victorian world picture; she rejected materialist science and orthodox religion with equal force. As an alternative, she built up a vision of the world that combined very nearly everything that had been rejected by the official science and scholarship of her time. Lost continents, secret societies, the claim that the works of William Shakespeare were actually written by Francis Bacon, theories of evolution in which animals were descended from man rather than vice versa, and much more along the same lines filled Blavatsky's massive works, along with a great deal of lore from the Western magical traditions and Eastern mysticism.

Blavatsky's version of occult history swept all before it, and for a century—from 1875 to 1975—there were few occult movements in the Western world that didn't include references to Atlantis, Lemuria, and the masters of the Great White Lodge somewhere in their instructional papers. The idea that these things were a central part of the occult tradition was rarely questioned.

In the last quarter of the twentieth century, however, a large number of occult movements began breaking away from the Theosophical version of occult history. In the Hermetic tradition and such related movements as Thelema, a rising interest in authentic knowledge about older systems of magic made occult history, with its shaky foundations in the realm of fact, less interesting. An increased focus on magical practice, as distinct from occult theory, in this wing of the community also fed into this change, as students of the occult found themselves wondering what the lore of Atlantis had to do with the practical work of magical training. In the Neopagan movement, by contrast, many people rejected the occult history of the Theosophists in order to build up a new and different version, in which ancient matriarchies and the survival of Pagan traditions over millennia played the central role.

Ironically, as large elements of the occult community were moving away from the Theosophical version of occult history, that version found a new audience in the burgeoning New Age movement. *SEE* NEW AGE MOVEMENT. Nearly all of the "secrets of the past" that were the stock in trade of occultists in the early twentieth century have been revamped and put back to work as elements of modern New Age ideology. There is thus every reason to think that occult history will be around for a long time to come.

octatopos: (Greek, "eight place") In ancient astrology, a system in which there were eight rather than twelve houses in the zodiac. The meanings were identical to the first eight houses of the modern house system. *SEE* HOUSE, ASTROLOGICAL.

Order of the Star in the East: *SEE* STAR IN THE EAST, ORDER OF THE.

ouroboros: (Greek, "tail biter") The serpent who swallows his own tail, a common image in magic and alchemy from ancient times to the present. It appears to be Egyptian in origin—for example, it appears in the tomb furnishings of Tutankhamen—but spread over much of the Western world by late classical times. It has had a variety of meanings. In alchemy, it has usually represented the process of circulation, in which a substance is distilled, the distillate poured back onto the residue, and the process repeated.

Paracelsus: (Philippus Aureolus Theophrastus Bombastus Paracelsus von Hohenheim) Swiss alchemist, physician, and occultist, 1493–1541. A physician's son from a remote mountain village in Switzerland, he grew up among miners and country folk, and developed early on a respect for traditional folklore and a contempt for established intellectual authorities. His mother died when he was nine, and his father relocated to Villach, in what is now part of Slovenia, where he found work teaching in the mining school. Young Theo von Hohenheim eagerly studied alchemy and mineralogy, and also attended monastic schools, where he gained a solid grounding in Latin.

At the age of fourteen, he left home to study, and in the usual fashion of the time attended several universities before receiving his bachelor's degree from the University of Vienna in 1511. He went on to medical school at the University of Ferrara, where he is thought to have received a medical degree around 1516. Thereafter he set out on a series of travels. Working as an army surgeon, he traveled through most of Europe, going east as far as central Asia, west to Spain and Britain, and south to Egypt. He finally returned to Villach in 1524, but set out almost immediately thereafter on another series of wanderings through central Europe.

A difficult, arrogant man with a severe alcohol problem, Paracelsus had a talent for alienating friends and making enemies, and as a result he was never able to settle anywhere for long. In 1526, as a result of his early publications and several notable cures, Paracelsus was appointed professor of medicine at the University of Basel, where he enlivened his lectures by publicly burning the works of Galen and Avicenna, the standard medical texts of the time. By 1528 he had quarreled so violently with the Basel city government that he had to escape from the town by night, and resumed his wandering life.

Much of his effort in the years that followed the Basel debacle was devoted to writing books expounding his theories of medicine, magic, and alchemy. Oporinus, his secretary at the time, commented: "He could not be found sober an hour or two together, in particular after his departure from Basel. Nevertheless, when he was most drunk and came home to dictate to me, he was so consistent and logical that a sober man could not have improved upon his manuscripts." His books went on to win a popularity he himself never managed. In 1540, his health failing, he settled in Salzburg, Austria, where he died of a stroke a year later while drinking at an inn.

Paracelsus was responsible for a massive reorientation of alchemy, one that has continued to the present. To him, the central purpose of alchemy was the creation of herbal and chemical medicines to cure disease. He became the founder of modern spagyrics, and his approaches to spagyric theory and practice are still standard today. In alchemical theory, he introduced the concept of the Three Principles: salt, sulphur, and mercury. His medical system, which was largely based on alchemy, saw the human body as an alchemical laboratory in which the *archeus*, the essential vital spirit centered in the stomach, transmuted food and drink into the substance of a human body.

Philosopher's Stone: The great goal of alchemical practice, the Philosopher's Stone or *medicina metallorum* ("medicine of metals") is a substance with the power to transmute base metals into pure gold. According to alchemical writings, it also has the power to cure all human diseases, to turn ordinary stones into gemstones, and to make glass flexible. It is described in Renaissance and early modern accounts as a fine but very heavy powder the color of rubies. The exact composition of the Philosopher's Stone is the supreme secret of practical alchemy.

Properly speaking, the Philosopher's Stone or Red Stone is only one, if the most important, of several different stones that are discussed in alchemical writings. The White Stone is an earlier result of the same process that produces the Red Stone, and has the power to turn base metals to pure silver. In spagyric or herbal alchemy, the vegetable stone is much discussed; it is a fixed substance that contains the highest possible level of healing virtue from the original plant. According to some writers, it also separates an herbal tincture into its three principles (the sulphur, salt, and mercury of the plant) without the difficult operations usually needed for the purpose.

Pike, Albert: American soldier, author, Freemason, and occultist, 1809–1891. Born in Massachusetts, the son of an alcoholic cobbler, he showed promise as a scholar from his childhood, learning Hebrew, Latin, and Greek in his teen years. He easily passed his entrance exams at Harvard but was unable to afford tuition, and in 1831 left Massachusetts for the frontier. Winding up in Fort Smith, Arkansas, he taught school for a time, edited a newspaper, and became a lawyer. In 1834 he married Ann Hamilton, and her money enabled him to go into politics. In 1846, during the Texas war of independence, he led a band of volunteers against the Mexican army at the battle of Buena Vista. He also found friends among the local Native American tribes and represented them in court against the federal government.

Pike became a Freemason during his time in Arkansas, and joined the Scottish Rite—at that time one of the smallest Masonic bodies, with fewer than a thousand members in the United States—in 1853. His scholarship and classical background led the Supreme Council of the Rite's Southern Jurisdiction to appoint him to a five-man committee charged with revising the rituals. The committee never met, but Pike took on the task himself, studying most of what was then known about the Western world's occult heritage in the process. His massive revision was complete in draft by 1859. That same year, with the resignation of Supreme Commander Albert Mackey, Pike became the head of the Southern Jurisdiction of the Scottish Rite.

When the Civil War began in 1861, he sided with the Confederacy and was appointed commissioner of Indian affairs by Jefferson Davis. Placed in command of Native units, with the rank of brigadier general, he found himself caught between loyalties when his Confederate superiors gave him orders he felt violated the treaty rights of his Native soldiers. In July of 1862 he resigned his command and published an open letter to the tribes accusing the Confederate government of ignoring its treaty obligations. In response, he was arrested and jailed, then released as the Confederacy's western defenses collapsed in the late fall of 1862.

Out of money, in constant danger from the soldiers of both sides, and with his marriage in ruins, Pike fled to a cabin in the Ozark hills with his books and remained there until 1868, intensively studying the Cabala, the Hindu and Zoroastrian scriptures, and what was known about the Gnostics. In the process, he revised the Scottish Rite rituals further, expanding them to include large portions of occult tradition.

In 1868 Pike left Arkansas for Washington, D.C., where he spent the rest of his life, living in a simple room paid for by the Supreme Council and devoting nearly all his time to the Scottish Rite, to other fraternal involvements, and to esoteric scholarship. He died in 1891. *SEE ALSO* FREEMASONRY.

Plato: (Aristocles of Athens) Greek philosopher, 427–347 BCE. The most influential philosopher in the history of the Western world, Plato was born in Athens to an aristocratic family that traced its descent to the last king of Athens; his actual name was Aristocles, but he was given the nickname Plato (Greek *platon*, "broad") because of the width of his shoulders. In his youth he was a noted athlete, competing in wrestling in the Isthmian Games at Corinth, and was educated as a poet and dramatist. At the age of twenty he encountered the philosopher Socrates, and became his chief disciple from that time until 399, when Socrates was executed by the Athenian government.

After Socrates' death, Plato went to Megara, where he studied philosophy together with his friend Euclid, who was later famous for his writings on geometry. From there he traveled around the Mediterranean world, visiting Egypt, Cyrene (in what is now Tunisia), Italy, and Sicily in search of philosophical wisdom. While in Sicily he offended the dictator of Syracuse, Dionysius, and was sold into slavery, but a friend found him in Aegina and bought his freedom. He then returned to Athens, where he founded his school, the Academy. Except for two later visits to Sicily, he remained in Athens, teaching and writing, for the rest of his life.

Plato was strongly influenced by his teacher Socrates, but also by the teachings of the Pythagorean school, and the philosophy he taught to his students at the Academy and wove into his writings was a fusion of the two. Certainly geometry and the other disciplines of the quadrivium were taught at the Academy, which had a sign over the door saying "Let no one ignorant of geometry enter here." *SEE* PYTHAGORAS; QUADRIVIUM.

References in ancient times to a set of "unwritten doctrines" passed on by lectures at the Academy suggest that the Pythagorean system came to be the theoretical core of his system, while Socrates' method of teaching by question and answer became the core method. Plato's dialogues, which have often been treated as detailed discussions of his own opinions, are literary works intended for a popular audience, and there is a great deal of scholarly debate about how much of Plato's developed philosophy they contain. *SEE* PLATONISM.

Plato's reputation has risen and fallen many times over the centuries between his time and the present, with some ages considering him the ideal philosopher and master of wisdom while others have dismissed him as a crackpot. His traditional birthday on November 8 is still celebrated by many Platonists with a feast.

Platonism: The philosophical movement founded by Plato, which lived on after him to become the single most influential philosophy in the history of the Western world. Platonism has powerfully influenced a wide range of Pagan, Jewish, Christian, Muslim, and nonreligious thinkers over more than two millennia. It also became far and away the most important philosophical basis for the Western occult traditions, and for two thousand years after Plato's time the vast majority of scholarly magic was grounded directly or indirectly on Platonist ideas about the universe.

Plato (427–347 BCE), the founder of Platonist philosophy, was heavily influenced by the earlier Pythagorean school and by a range of earlier Greek philosophers. *SEE* PYTHAGORAS. He saw the central problem of philosophy as the relation between the ever-changing world perceived by the senses—the realm of Becoming, in his terms—and the timeless realities of the spirit, the realm of Being. The core of his philosophy was the concept that everything perceived by the senses is a reflection or projection of some essential pattern in the realm of Being. He called these essential patterns Forms or Ideas, and taught that given the right forms of training, they could be experienced directly by the human mind.

During his lifetime, Plato founded a school, the Academy, that carried on his teachings and developed his philosophy for centuries after his death. At first centered on the Academy in Athens, Platonism gradually spread more widely, and by the beginning of the Common Era had adherents throughout the Mediterranean world. One of these, Philo of Alexandria (c. 20 BCE–after 39 CE), launched the tradition on a trajectory that would have important consequences for the future. Philo was a Jew, a member of one of Alexandria's most prominent Jewish families, and he set himself the goal of making sense of Jewish scriptures and traditions in the light of Platonic philosophy. The result was successful enough to give rise to many later projects along the same lines, fusing Platonism not only with Judaism but also with Christianity and Islam. The same broad diffusion of Platonist ideas that led to Philo's project also found its way into occult circles.

Pythagoras and some of his successors had probably been magicians in every sense of the word, and although Plato was deeply suspicious of magical practices, his philosophy was quickly put to use by magicians as a way of making sense of their own traditions. The *Chaldean Oracles* of Julianus the Theurgist, a major magical text of the early Common Era, is deeply imbued with Platonist ideas. Similarly, Platonism found its way into a range of spiritual traditions closely related to the occultism of the time. Both Gnosticism and Hermeticism were deeply influenced by Platonism; in fact, a section of Plato's dialogue *The Republic*, translated into Coptic, was included by one sect of ancient Gnostics in the holy books of the Nag Hammadi library. *SEE* GNOSTICISM; HERMETICISM.

In the early third century CE, Platonism underwent a major shift with the appearance of Plotinus (c. 205–270 CE), who became effectively the second founder of the tradition. In his essays, collected after his death by his disciple Porphyry of Tyre as *The Enneads*, he reworked Plato's vision of the worlds of Being and Becoming into a system of four worlds. In his thought, the realm of Becoming was divided into the hylic world, or world of matter, and the psychic world, or world of ordinary consciousness, while the realm of Being was separated into the noetic world, the level of the Forms, and the henadic world, the level of the ultimate unity behind all things. A mystic and a visionary, Plotinus began what modern scholars call the Neoplatonist movement, which turned Platonism more directly toward the realms of spirituality and the occult. By the time of Plotinus, a new force—Christianity—was beginning to make itself felt in the Roman world, and Platonism became one of the major centers of opposition to the new creed. Plotinus' student Porphyry wrote a book titled *Against the Christians,* every copy of which was destroyed after Christianity seized power in the fourth century. On a wider scale was the project of Iamblichus of Chalcis (died 330), the great fourth century Platonist, who set out to redefine Platonism as the foundation of a unified Paganism that could resist Christian inroads. Proclus (412–485), the last great Pagan Platonist of the ancient world, drew on Iamblichus' work in devising a Pagan Platonist theology that made room for every aspect of traditional Pagan practice.

Iamblichus and Proclus, like most Platonists in the last two centuries of the ancient world, were followers of a new tradition in Platonism, the theurgical tradition. Theurgists combined philosophical study with magical and religious ritual; they taught that just as the rational side of the self needed to be trained through logic and philosophy, the nonrational side needed to be purified and healed through ritual means. Nearly all the major defenders of Paganism in the classical world's final centuries were deeply involved in theurgy. *SEE* THEURGY.

Ironically, though, the same Platonist ideas that were being used by Iamblichus and Proclus to illuminate traditional Pagan rites were also being used, at the same time, by a handful of Christian philosophers and theologians to make sense of their very different tradition. Origen (185–254), an important Christian thinker of the third century, was a fellow-student of Plotinus in the Platonic schools of Alexandria; he was only one of a series of Christian Platonists who shaped what would be a major influence on Christian theology and philosophy. Among the most important of these was an anonymous writer who called himself Dionysius the Areopagite (c. sixth century CE). Pseudo-Dionysius, as he is usually called, replaced Pagan gods with Christian angels to rework Proclus' theurgical Platonism into a system that was central to most Christian mysticism until the time of the Reformation a thousand years later. Largely because of its adoption by Christianity, Platonism was essentially the only classical philosophy to survive the fall of Rome in a living form. In the Byzantine Empire, centered on Constantinople (modern

Istanbul), the works of Plato and his followers remained in circulation, and the Eastern Orthodox Church drew heavily on Platonism as it developed its theology and philosophy. To this day a very strong Platonist streak can be traced in all the Orthodox churches. Western Europe was another matter. Greek was for all practical purposes a lost language in the West, and the Latin Platonist writings that survived the fall of Rome were fairly meager: a partial Latin translation of Plato's dialogue *Timaeus* survived, along with a few other texts by later writers. On the other hand, many of the early Christian Platonists were central to the learning of the early medieval Catholic Church. Crucial figures included Augustine, bishop of Hippo in North Africa (354–430 CE), far and away the most influential theologian of the age; Martianus Capella (fifth century CE), whose encyclopedic *Marriage of Philology and Mercury* was the most popular textbook of the liberal arts well into the high Middle Ages; and pseudo-Dionysius the Aropagite, mentioned earlier in this article. These were all Platonists of one sort or another, and their writings provided the core resources drawn on by early medieval philosophers.

For the first four centuries or so after the fall of Rome, philosophers of any sort were few and far between in the West; in an age of drastic instability and violence, most scholars were concerned with preserving and passing on the basic elements of education, and with Christian theology. With the rise of a more stable society after Charlemagne (742–814 CE), the founder of the Holy Roman Empire, opportunities for scholarship broadened. John Scotus Eriugena (ninth century CE), the first great medieval Platonist, taught at the court of Charles the Bald, king of France, and produced a series of important works and translations from Greek into Latin; he was familiar with most of the important Platonist works and attempted, with mixed results, to introduce Platonist ideas into the Christianity of his time. After him came a long and distinguished line of Christian Platonists, who developed most of what is now classified as early medieval philosophy along Platonist lines.

The tradition of Christian Platonism was eclipsed in the twelfth and thirteenth centuries, though, by the rediscovery of Aristotle's writings, which were translated out of Arabic into Latin starting in the middle of the twelfth century. Aristotle's rationalist thought won wide acceptance in educated circles and even, once it was Christianized by Thomas Aquinas, in the church itself. Platonism, and mysticism generally, remained influential in the Franciscan Order and in a few other contexts, but it remained for the Renaissance to tip the balance back. At the same time as Platonist thought was losing influence in the Christian world, however, it played an important role in launching a major new movement in Judaism. Jewish mystical circles in the south of France in the eleventh century were strongly influenced by Platonist writings, as well as by older Jewish mystical systems—the Ma'aseh Berashith, or "Work of Creation," and the Ma'aseh Merkabahor, "Work of the Chariot." The fusion of these teachings, primarily in the circle of Isaac the Blind (died c. 1235 CE), gave rise to the Cabala; SEE CABALA. It was not until the fifteenth century, however, that Platonism rose back into widespread prominence in the West. The coming of the Renaissance awakened a renewed interest in ancient philosophy, and the recovery of the complete works of Plato—first translated from Greek to Latin by the Florentine scholar and occultist Marsilio Ficino (1433–1499)—spurred a widespread fad for Platonism.

Over the next century and a half, most of the other classics of Platonist thought came back into circulation. At the same time, both Hermeticism and the Cabala entered scholarly circles across Europe; the *Corpus Hermeticum* had been translated by Ficino just before Plato, and Ficino's younger contemporary Giovanni Pico della Mirandola (1463–1494) was responsible for publicizing the Cabala. SEE CORPUS HERMETICUM; HERMETICISM. Scholars across Europe quickly recognized the connections among these traditions—and the links that tied all of them to occult theory and practice. The result was Renaissance Hermeticism, a widely popular and intensely magical way of thought that drew its theology from the Cabala and the Christian Platonists of earlier centuries, its mythology from Hermeticism, and its philosophy straight from Platonism by way of Plotinus and the late classical theurgists. It played a dominant role in most of the major occult works of the time. Widely influential, it was also bitterly attacked by its opponents, and it became one of the major forces in an age of free-wheeling intellectual warfare.

By the end of the sixteenth century, the intellectual battle lines hardened into a three-way struggle among Renaissance Hermeticism, the scholastic Aristotelianism of the universities, and the first formulations of what was then called "the mechanical philosophy" and is now called modern scientific materialism. Over the century that followed, the last of these gradually won out in the West. Platonism underwent one last major revival in the seventeenth century, when the Cambridge Platonists in England turned to Christian Platonism as a weapon against materialist philosophies. Henry More (1614–1687), the leading light of the movement, and a number of others struggled to defend the reality of the spiritual, and managed at least to ensure that Christian Platonism would remain a viable option within the Anglican Church.

The Cambridge Platonist revival faded out in the early eighteenth century, and thereafter the "mechanical philosophy" of Descartes, Bacon, and Newton held the field. For most of the following three centuries Platonism was largely ignored in the Western world, except by scholars and educated occultists. One major exception was Thomas Taylor (1758–1835), the great English Platonist and Pagan, who translated nearly all the surviving Platonist writings from ancient Greek into English. His efforts played a central role in launching the Neopagan revival in nineteenth-century Britain, which was directly ancestral to the modern Pagan movement, and he was also a major source drawn on by the Transcendentalists in America. Taylor's translations and his bold promotion of a Platonized Paganism as "the true religion of mankind" found few takers in the occult community of his time, however, and the reading lists offered by magical orders of the next century or so include essentially none of the standard Platonist canon. The same general neglect of Platonism in occult circles has continued to the present. It remains to be seen whether Western occultism has finally broken with what was once its core philosophy, or whether occultists of some future time will once again draw on Platonism as a resource for their work.

Plotinus: Greek-Egyptian philosopher, c. 205–270 CE. Plotinus was the most important and influential philosopher of the Neoplatonic school. Little is known about his early life, as he preferred not to talk about himself. According to the biography written by his student Porphyry of Tyre, he was a native of Egypt; he decided to devote himself to philosophy at the age of twenty-eight, and after a time he spent visiting different teachers spent eleven years studying with the Neoplatonist Ammonius in Alexandria. In 243, hoping to travel into the East, he accompanied the army of the Emperor Gordian on a military expedition against the Persians. Gordian was assassinated by his own soldiers, and Plotinus escaped with some difficulty and made his way to Rome, where he began teaching publicly in 244. He remained in Rome until shortly before his death. His pupil Porphyry later collected and edited his writings into a single volume, *The Enneads*, which became the single most important source for later Platonist thought.

Plotinus himself was a mystic rather than a magician, and saw no need for ritual or symbolic methods in the quest for inner transformation; in his view, ethical virtue and disciplined reasoning were all that was needed. On the other hand, his writings assume the effectiveness of magic and present an explanation for its powers that later, more magically oriented Platonists found useful. His philosophical system became central to nearly all later approaches to Platonism, and also played an important role in the development of esoteric Christian traditions. *SEE ALSO* PLATONISM.

Pythagoras: Greek philosopher and mathematician, c. 570–c. 495 BCE. According to the four ancient accounts of his life, Pythagoras was a native of Samos, but left his homeland as a young man in search of knowledge. After studying philosophy with Thales of Miletus and Pherecydes of Syros, he is said to have traveled to Egypt, Babylonia, and several other countries, where he studied traditional religious and mystical lore with priests in a variety of temples. He then emigrated to Crotona, a Greek colonial city in southern Italy, where he spent most of the rest of his life. In Crotona he founded a secret society, later known as the Pythagorean Brotherhood, which passed on his teachings and also played an important role in the political life of the community. Around 500 BCE, popular unrest over the brotherhood's political influence led to widespread rioting, and many of the brotherhood were killed. Pythagoras himself fled to Metapontum, where he died a few years later

The teachings Pythagoras brought with him to Crotona were communicated under vows of secrecy, and there has been much dispute ever since about just what they included. Accounts in classical literature credit Pythagoras with discoveries in mathematics, geometry, and music theory, but also with miracles of the type claimed for other ancient magicians, such as Apollonius of Tyana. Belief in reincarnation, insistence on a vegetarian diet, a detailed system of number mysticism, and a variety of moral and philosophical maxims were also ascribed to him by ancient sources.

In many ways Pythagoras can be seen as the founder, or at least the first historical figure, of Western occult tradition. Certainly many of the factors central to his biography—the search for wisdom in exotic countries, the idea that a secret initiatory society is the proper context for esoteric teachings, the fatal lure of political involvement—as well as many of the specific teachings attributed to him have remained standard features of occultism in the West ever since his time. *SEE ALSO* ARITHMANCY; QUADRIVIUM; SACRED GEOMETRY.

quadrivium: (Latin, "four roads") The four ancient sciences of number, usually listed as arithmetic, geometry, music, and astronomy. These categories should not be understood in a purely scientific mode, however. "Arithmetic" in earlier times included a great deal of number symbolism, and what would now be called arithmology and arithmancy, "geometry" included the sort of mystical perspectives now classified as sacred geometry; "music" included all the arts, and focused primarily on harmonious number relationships; and "astronomy" included not merely astrology but also the various ways of tracking the cycles of time.

The sciences that later became the quadrivium were first formulated in the Western world by the Pythagorean Brotherhood, which drew on older Egyptian and Mesopotamian lore, and were organized into a set of four in the late classical period. By the dawn of the Middle Ages, the quadrivium was enshrined as the second stage of a liberal education, following the trivium, which consisted of Latin grammar, logic, and rhetoric. The trivium and quadrivium formed the seven liberal arts, and remained central to education throughout the Western world until the dawn of the modern age. They played a particularly important role in Renaissance occultism, and it may have been because of this connection that the quadrivium fell into neglect after the triumph of materialist philosophies in the seventeenth century. *SEE ALSO* ARITHMOLOGY; ASTROLOGY; PYTHAGORAS; SACRED GEOMETRY.

Rosencreutz, Christian: Legendary founder of the Rosicrucian order (1378–1484). The *Fama Fraternitatis*, the first of the original Rosicrucian documents, is the only source concerning his biography, and refers to him throughout simply as C. R. or C. R. C. His full name was first published in the *Chemical Wedding of Christian Rosenkreutz*, the third of the documents. His name has been variously spelled; the spelling used in this entry is the most common.

According to the *Fama*'s account, Rosencreutz was born in Germany to a noble but penniless family. At the age of five he entered a monastery, where he learned Greek and Latin. While still in his teens, he eagerly set out on a pilgrimage to the Holy Land with an elder brother of the same monastery, whose initials were P. A. L.

The journey was interrupted by the death of P. A. L. in Cyprus, but Rosencreutz was unwilling to turn back and continued to Damascus, hoping to go on from there to Jerusalem. He was prevented from doing so "by reason of the feebleness of his body"—although the same source later comments on his strong constitution—and won favor with the Turks in Damascus because of his skill in medicine.

While in Damascus, he learned of Damear (modern Dhamar), a city of wise men in Arabia, where wonders were wrought and the secrets of nature disclosed. Changing his travel plans, he paid a group of Arabs to take him to Damear. There, according to the *Fama*, the inhabitants greeted him as though they had long expected him, called him by his name, and showed him secrets from the monastery where he had grown up. He stayed in Damear for three years, studying medicine and mathematics, and improving his command of Arabic. Then he traveled by way of Egypt to the city of Fez, where he spent two years studying magic and Cabala.

Completing his studies, he went to Spain, hoping to share what he had learned with the scholars of Europe. This hope was disappointed, and his discoveries were rejected and laughed at, not only in Spain but elsewhere in Europe. So, finally, Rosencreutz returned to Germany where, after five years of further studies, he sought out three brothers from his old monastery and with them formed the Fraternity of the Rosy Cross. Four more, one of them Rosencreutz' nephew, were brought into the fraternity at a later time. While the majority of the brethren traveled throughout the world, Rosencreutz remained at the headquarters of the fraternity, the Collegium Spiritus Sancti, until the time of his death, and was buried there in a concealed underground vault. The rediscovery of this vault and of Rosencreutz' uncorrupted body in 1604 was the occasion for the publication of the Rosicrucian manifestoes, and became the central narrative of the movement.

The second of the original documents, the *Confessio Fraternitatis*, adds nothing of substance to the biography just given. The third, the *Chemical Wedding*, is a complex alchemical fable narrated by Rosencreutz in the first person, but its relationship to the figure described in the *Fama* is uncertain.

There have been various efforts to argue that Rosencreutz was an actual historical figure. Some Theosophists claimed him as an earlier incarnation of the Comte de Saint Germain, and a painting by Rembrandt "The Polish Rider," painted c. 1655—has been identified as a portrait either of the Comte or of Rosencreutz himself. Other writers have proposed that Paracelsus or the Polish alchemist Michael Sendivogius were the original on which the portrait of Rosencreutz was based. Such claims are hard to disprove but have little evidence to support them. *SEE ALSO* ROSICRUCIANS.

Rosicrucians: In Western occult tradition, a secret order of adepts using the symbol of the Rose Cross. Many different groups and teachers have claimed the Rosicrucian legacy over the years, creating a thick cloud of confusion around the subject. The first mention of the Rosicrucian Order dates from the year 1614, when a booklet was published by Wilhelm Wessel in the German city of Cassel. The full title of the booklet is worth quoting: *Universal and General Reformation of the Whole Wide World; together with the Fama Fraternitatis of the Praiseworthy Fraternity of the Rosy Cross, written to all the Learned and Rulers of Europe; also a short reply sent by Herr Haselmayer, for which he was seized by the Jesuits and condemned to a galley; now put into print and communicated to all true hearts.* The first part of this booklet, the "Universal and General Reformation," is a German translation of one chapter of Traiano Boccalini's *Ragguagli di Parnasso* (1612); this is a scathing satire in which Apollo sets out to reform the world, listens to the harebrained schemes of a variety of wise men, and finally limits his reform to new laws governing the price of vegetables. There follows the *Fama Fraternitatis*, or "Announcement of the Fraternity," which proclaims the existence of a secret Fraternity of the Rose Cross, describes the life of its founder Christian Rosencreutz and the discovery of the vault in which he and many of the secrets of the fraternity were buried, and invites all like-minded people to contact the Fraternity and share in its wisdom and alchemical wealth. The final item, Herr Haselmayer's letter, is an attempt to make contact with the order.

The *Fama*'s publication ignited an extraordinary furor all over Europe. Conservatives denounced the mysterious order, skeptics questioned its existence, Hermeticists defended it, and plenty of people tried to take it up on its offer of membership. Books, pamphlets, broadsheets, letters, and other publications on the subject came from presses all over Europe.

A second pamphlet emerged in 1615 from the same press. This was titled *A Short Consideration of the More Secret Philosophy, written by Philip à Gabella, student of Philosophy, now published for the first time along with the Confession of the R. C. Fraternity*. The "Short Consideration" was an essay on magical philosophy based on John Dee's *Monas Hieroglyphica* (1564); the *Confessio*, which followed it, expanded on the material in the *Fama* from a somewhat more doctrinaire Lutheran standpoint.

A year later, with the controversy still at full boil, the third "manifesto"—titled *Chymische Hochzeit Christiani Rosenkreutz Anno 1549* (The Chemical Wedding of Christian Rosencreutz, Year 1549)—was published by Lazarus Zetzner, a Strasburg printer. Not actually a manifesto at all, the *Chemical Wedding* is an alchemical and allegorical fable, narrated in the first person by Christian Rosencreutz himself, which describes his journey to visit the wedding of a mysterious king and queen and the pomp and complex ceremonies that surround this event, culminating in the death and resurrection of the bride and bridegroom.

All three of these original publications were issued anonymously. The third, the *Chemical Wedding*, was apparently the first one to be written, and its author was Johann Valentin Andreae. In later life a sober Lutheran minister, Andreae was a college student at the time he wrote the *Chemical Wedding*, involved in Hermeticist circles at the University of Tübingen; his father and brother were both alchemists. In his autobiography, which he wrote late in life and which remained unpublished until 1799, he admitted to having written the *Chemical Wedding* a few years after beginning his studies at Tübingen in 1601; an entry in another of his writings fixes the date of authorship as 1605. Its publication in 1616 occurred at the hands of a "false brother," according to Andreae's account, and occasioned Andreae a good deal of embarrassment; he had been appointed to his first church post only two years before, and was busy trying to put the more scandalous parts of his college career behind him. Additional evidence supports this account, and Andreae's authorship of the Chemical Wedding is accepted by virtually all scholars.

The *Fama* and *Confessio* are a more complex affair. While Andreae may have had a hand in them and certainly knew the people involved, he was not acting alone.

At the time when they were written (c. 1608–1610), Andreae was a member of a circle of Christian Hermeticists around the Paracelsian physician Tobias Hess (1568–1614), and—again, by way of comments in one of Andreae's writings—we know that Hess wrote at least part of the *Confessio.* The two manifestos may be by a number of authors working together, a common practice at the time.

The purpose of the two manifestos has given rise to endless speculation, but an important clue in the matter has received too little attention. The *Fama*, the first of the manifestos, did not appear alone; it was published with a translation of an Italian satire. (The translation itself was made by Christoph Besold, another important Hermeticist in Tübingen and a close friend of Andreae's.) *The General Reformation* is a mordant mythological satire on schemes of social reform; it is followed by a manifesto proclaiming, among other things, a mythological scheme for social reform. It's hard to miss the implication that the entire project was intended as a joke.

Certainly this was Andreae's opinion. He referred to the Rosicrucian writings consistently in later years as a *ludibrium*, a word that can mean "joke," "comedy," "play," or "mockery." In one of his writings (*Mythologiae Christiana*, 1618) he makes a curious comment about the "comedy" having involved "an entire change of actors." This is apparently what happened. What had started out within

Andreae's circle of friends had spun out of their control
within a short time of the first publication. What began
as an ornate joke, of the sort much practiced at the time,
became something (or, rather, several somethings) much
more serious. Writers unconnected with the original circle began to borrow the Rosicrucian symbolism and story
as a framework for Lutheranism, alchemical and magical
teachings, or millennarian prophecies of the approaching
end of the world.

There also seems to have been a political dimension,
one that would have disastrous consequences. While the
original manifestos were being written, a complex political intrigue centering on Friedrich V, Prince Palatine of
the Rhine, was coming to fruition. Friedrich was one of
the leading lights among the Protestant monarchs of the
period. Rudolf II, king of Bohemia and Holy Roman Emperor, had abdicated in 1611, and his successor Matthias
died only five years later. Since the Bohemian crown was
elective, not hereditary, Friedrich's advisers and supporters were busily positioning him as future king of Bohemia, with the imperial crown a tantalizing possibility. The
scheme failed catastrophically; Friedrich was crowned
king of Bohemia in 1619, but he and his allies were over-
whelmed by Catholic armies in the Battle of the White
Mountain in 1620. The Palatinate was overrun later the

same year, and Friedrich was driven into lifelong exile in Holland.

Under Friedrich, the Palatinate of the Rhine had become a major center not only of Lutheranism but of Hermetic and alchemical influences. Not only the Rosicrucian manifestos but other Hermetic publications of the same period may have played a part in a deliberate propaganda scheme to foster a Lutheran-Hermetic movement backing Friedrich and opposing the House of Habsburg, the champions of the Catholic reaction. The Thirty Years War, which broke out in the aftermath of Friedrich's failed gamble, effectively ended the German occult revival of the period, and whatever might have been behind the Rosicrucian manifestoes seems to have gone into hiding or out of existence at that time. Only in England and the Scandinavian countries, where the Catholic Church had definitively lost power decades earlier, did writers who aligned themselves with the Rosicrucian movement remain active. Even there, the movement (if it was a movement) seems to have petered out by the end of the seventeenth century.

The resurgence of Rosicrucian orders in the next century was set in motion by the spread of Freemasonry, which emerged from obscurity in England in the second decade of the eighteenth century and spread to most European countries within a few decades afterward. As Masonic initiates began adding to the three original degrees of Entered Apprentice, Fellow Craft, and Master Mason, nearly all the traditional secret societies and Mystery cults of the past were ransacked for inspiration, and Rosicrucianism was not exempt. The result was a flurry of Masonic Rosicrucian orders from the eighteenth century to the present. *SEE* FREEMASONRY.

Similar motives in the massive occult renaissance of the late nineteenth and early twentieth centuries gave rise to a new outpouring of Rosicrucian organizations. The Hermetic Order of the Golden Dawn in England and the Rose+Croix Kabbalistique in France, which between them played a dominant role in the turn-of-the-century European occult scene, claimed Rosicrucian lineage and made much use of Rosicrucian symbolism. "Sâr" Josephin Peladan, whose occult-inspired art shows were the toast of late nineteenth-century Paris, drew on the same source.

In the first decades of the twentieth century, America saw the rise of a series of large-scale Rosicrucian magical orders that operated on the correspondence-course principle, and taught the basics of occult philosophy and practice to two generations of American magicians. Another twentieth-century addition to the Rosicrucian ranks was Austrian occultist Rudolf Steiner (1861–1925), who made use of Rosicrucian traditions in his voluminous writings on occult theory and practice. The Rosicrucian tradition even has a place in the prehistory of modern Wicca. Further Rosicrucian developments can probably be expected in the twenty-first century as well.

In the last two centuries, in keeping with the grand occult tradition of falsifying history, various accounts of the origins of Rosicrucianism have been circulated tracing it back to ancient Egypt, Atlantis, or some similarly remote period; at least one currently active Rosicrucian order claims that the tradition dates back to the heretic pharaoh Akhenaten in the fourteenth century BCE. *SEE AKHENATEN*. Sadly, these claims have no trace of historical evidence to back them, and represent yet another offshoot of the rich legacy of occult pseudo-history. *SEE OCCULT HISTORY. SEE ALSO* FLUDD, ROBERT; ROSENCREUTZ, CHRISTIAN.

runes: (Old Norse *run*, "secret") A group of ancient alphabets used by Germanic and Scandinavian peoples as a system of writing for practical purposes and as a magical and divinatory tool. The oldest known system of runes, the elder futhark of twenty-four letters, apparently originated sometime before 50 CE, the date of the oldest known runic artifact. (The term "futhark," used for a runic alphabet, is made up of the sound-values of the first six letters.) An expanded version, the Anglo-Saxon futhorc of either twenty-nine or thirty-three letters, was in use by 400 CE.

Among the peoples of Scandinavia, by contrast, the runic alphabet evolved in the other direction, simplifying into the younger futhark of sixteen runes.

Scholars have argued for more than a century about the origin of the runes, with Greek, Latin, and Etruscan alphabets being suggested as the original source of the runic letters. It's clear, however, that runes were deeply connected with Germanic magical traditions from the beginning, as the meaning of "rune" suggests.

The Roman historian Tacitus, in his account of the German tribes (the *Germania*, written in 98 CE), mentioned in passing a system of divination using *notae* ("signs"). Pieces of wood from a nut-bearing tree were marked with the *notae*, and three of these were drawn and interpreted. The first known runic artifact, a brooch found at Meldorf in Germany, dates from around 50 CE, so Tacitus' comment may be a reference to runic (or proto-runic) divination.

Later runic inscriptions, including the impressive rune-stones found across southern Scandinavia, also include magical words of power and long, incomprehensible passages similar to the *nomina barbara* of contemporary magic further south. Norse sagas and other written material from the last years of the runic tradition present the runes as magical through and through, and the god Odin is credited with their discovery. Runemasters, called *erilar* in the time of the elder futhark, apparently played a major role in the magical and spiritual life of the Germanic tribespeople of the Age of Migrations (c. 300–c. 800 CE), as their later Norse equivalents did until the Christianization of Scandinavia in the eleventh century.

With the coming of Christianity and the Latin alphabet, the runes gradually dropped out of use. Runic inscriptions from the Middle Ages often include elements from classical, Arabic, and medieval magical traditions, showing that the native magic of the north was fading out of memory. By the beginning of the Renaissance, rune lore survived only in fragmentary form in a handful of manuscript sources.

The rediscovery of the runes began with the work of the great Renaissance scholar and magician Johannes Bureus (1568–1652) in Sweden, who put the tools of contemporary classical scholarship to work on the surviving relics of Pagan Scandinavian culture. Remnants of Anglo-Saxon runic lore also caught the attention of English antiquaries from the Renaissance onwards.

The revival of the runes as a major presence in the Western occult tradition, however, began with the work of Guido von List (1848–1919), the seminal figure in the modern Teutonic revival. In 1902, while recovering from an eye operation, List underwent a mystical experience in which the runes played an important part. Out of this experience, he devised a somewhat idiosyncratic system of eighteen runes based on a passage from the *Elder Eddain* in which the god Odin recounts the runes' secret powers. This system remains popular in the German-speaking countries, but has had little following in the rest of the world. Another dominant figure in German runic studies was Friedrich Marby (1882–1966), who developed a method of runic yoga as part of a complex and impressive system of rune mysticism and magic.

Rune studies in the English-speaking world, on the other hand, progressed little until the rise of the first major Teutonic Pagan movements in the early 1970s, and remained a concern of very few for some years thereafter. The publication of Ralph Blum's *The Book of Runes* in 1978 changed this situation. While Blum's work has been harshly criticized as shallow and inaccurate, it served to introduce the runes to a widespread audience and created a market for more substantial studies of rune lore. The decades since that time have seen a flowering of rune studies, in conjunction with the development and spread of the Teutonic Pagan revival.

sacred geometry: In modern occult circles, the most common term for the branch of occult theory and practice focusing on geometrical form as a way of symbolizing, experiencing, and contacting spiritual levels of existence. A complex and erudite branch of occultism, sacred geometry is among the least well-known of occult traditions nowadays, although there has been a steady subcurrent of interest in it for many centuries.

In essence, sacred geometry is simply geometry as it was practiced throughout the Western world from ancient times until the coming of the Scientific Revolution. In ancient, medieval, and Renaissance times, geometrical forms and relationships were seen as an expression of the deep, archetypal structure of reality, and students of geometry were taught to experience geometric processes as the unfolding, in space and time, of spiritual realities.

These same patterns could equally be put to work in architecture and art. According to the theory of sacred geometry, when this is done, the spiritual force represented by the geometries of a building or an artwork affects people who encounter it, whether or not they know how to interpret the geometrical language. Greek temples and Gothic cathedrals, both of which were designed and built using the canons of sacred geometry, provide evidence of how well this works in practice. The history of sacred geometry in the Western occult tradition begins with Pythagoras of Samos (c. 570–c. 495 BCE), who traveled to Egypt and Babylon to study mathematics and philosophy, and founded a semisecret society that taught geometry as a spiritual discipline. *SEE* PYTHAGORAS. His followers, who scattered across the Mediterranean world in the aftermath of the anti-Pythagorean riots of the early fifth century BCE, took his geometrical lore with them.

Vitruvius, the one important Roman writer on architecture whose book survived the Middle Ages, quotes Pythagorean geometrical lore extensively. The masons' guilds of the Middle Ages, from which Freemasonry is descended, also preserved a great deal of what is now sacred geometry; *SEE* FREEMASONRY. The Christian church found that older traditions of sacred geometry could easily be converted to Christian use, and there is some reason to think that geometrical and mathematical symbolism are woven into many passages in the New Testament itself. Until the

Reformation—and well after it, in some areas—churches were universally designed and built with an eye to geometrical symbolism. *SEE* CHRISTIAN OCCULTISM.

A combination of traditional masons' lore and rediscovered classical documents came together in the Renaissance to launch a massive revival of sacred geometry. Internationally famous scholars such as the Venetian friar Francesco Giorgi (1466–1540) published important works on the subject, most of which have never been translated out of Latin. The practical applications of geometry were not neglected; Giorgi was a consultant on architectural symbolism, and a century later the renowned Dutch swordsman Gerard Thibault (1574–1629) published a book expounding an effective system of swordsmanship based on sacred geometry.

Like most branches of the Western occult traditions, sacred geometry fell on hard times with the coming of the Scientific Revolution. It was preserved mostly in the more occult end of Freemasonry, which kept enough contact with its roots to retain a fascination with geometrical symbolism. Several important books on sacred geometry and related principles were published in the eighteenth and nineteenth centuries, of which William Stirling's *The Canon* (1897) was the most influential.

The modern revival of sacred geometry began with the work of one man, René "Aour" Schwaller de Lubicz

(1887–1961), whose studies of Gothic cathedrals and ancient Egyptian monuments led him to an intensive study of traditional geometry and the publication of a series of massive and difficult books on the subject. Later, in the late 1960s and early 1970s, a number of English writers studying leys and earth mysteries came across Stirling's *The Canon* and similar works, and began work along similar lines. The current revival is fairly modest but has produced a number of excellent books and several beautifully designed buildings.

In earlier times, sacred geometry was considered to be part of the quadrivium, the four branches of occult mathematics. *SEE* ARITHMOLOGY; QUADRIVIUM.

sacrifice: The primary religious ritual of ancient Pagan religions, in which offerings—most often, though not always, livestock—were made at the altar of one or more gods. In the case of the livestock, the god or gods received a part of the offering, while the rest was generally cooked and shared amongst the worshippers. Other forms of sacrifice included throwing valuables into bodies of water or casting them down wells or ritual pits.

Detailed information on sacrificial rituals in ancient Greece and Rome has survived in classical literature. These, together with scattered information and archeological finds from the rest of Europe, and cross-cultural parallels from other Indo-European cultures such as ancient Persia and Vedic India, have allowed the Pagan sacrificial rituals of other Western cultures to be reconstructed in some detail.

The basic theory of ancient sacrifice was summed up concisely by the Romans in the phrase *do ut des*—"I give that you might give." Sacrifice was part of an exchange of gifts between the gods and humanity; the gods gave fertility to crops and livestock, and people gave back a portion of these things in exchange. Besides grain and livestock, other items of value might be offered; most of the Pagan religions of the Mediterranean basin made use of incense as an offering, for example, while the ancient Celts were famous for throwing gold and silver into rivers and lakes as offerings to their deities.

Sacrifice was also closely connected to divination. The entrails of livestock who were offered to the gods were inspected by diviner priests, who read them—especially the liver, which was associated with sky gods such as Jupiter—as an omen of the gods' response to the offering. This practice was known variously as haruspicy, hieromancy, or hepatoscopy. The behavior of the flames during the burning of any burnt offering was also watched as an omen. The movements of incense smoke and the crackling of grain offerings in the fire were also used to judge whether or not the gods had accepted the offering.

In Judaism, sacrificial rituals very similar to those of their Pagan neighbors were practiced up until the final destruction of the Temple of Jerusalem in 70 CE, and details of the rituals can still be found in the Old Testament and its Jewish commentaries. Much of the symbolism of Christianity is actually based on these ancient ritual forms, with Jesus of Nazareth playing the role of sacrificial lamb.

The rise of the Christian church to dominance in the last years of the classical period saw older traditions of sacrifice suppressed in most of the Western world. At first, this was justified by the idea that the sacrifice of Jesus had made all further sacrifice unnecessary. Later, in the Middle Ages, Christian theologians redefined "sacrifice" as the act of giving up some form of pleasure in order to prove how much one loves God. This would have been incomprehensible to a Pagan Roman, who might have wondered what benefit a god could get from watching a worshipper make himself or herself miserable; nonetheless, it remains a very common understanding (or misunderstanding).

Very few branches of the modern Neopagan revival have made much use of traditional ideas of sacrifice. Among the exceptions are some Norse and Celtic Reconstructionist groups, and a handful of Druid groups such as Ar nDraiocht Fein (ADF). The offerings used in these groups consist of grain, alcoholic beverages, cooked food, and jewelry, along with songs and poetry. A few groups have gone to the extent of baking imitation animals of bread and offering these up in an imitation of the time-honored fashion.

Scottish Rite: *SEE* FREEMASONRY.

self-initiation: A process by which a person who does not have access to formal ritual initiation, or who chooses not to seek initiation for some reason, carries out an approximation of the same process on his or her own.

In self-initiation, solo ritual work and a variety of training exercises replace the more traditional initiation rituals conferred by a group. The validity of self-initiation has been hotly disputed in some circles, but the practice has become a standard part of the current occult scene. A wide range of books outlining methods of self-initiation in different traditions are in print as of this writing. The emergence of the solitary practitioner as an important element of the modern magical and Pagan scene has helped to drive the popularity of self-initiation practices. *SEE ALSO* INITIATION.

Sephiroth: (Hebrew, "numerations") In Cabala, the ten emanations of God forming the Cabalistic Tree of Life; the singular form of the word is Sephirah. The doctrine of the Sephiroth is at the core of the Cabala, and forms the chief element that distinguishes the Cabala from earlier forms of Jewish mysticism such as the Ma'aseh Berashith and Ma'aseh Merkabah.

The original idea of ten special powers or manifestations of the divine is older than the Cabala, and both this idea and the term "Sephiroth" itself appear in the Sepher Yetzirah, a very ancient text that probably derives from the Ma'aseh Berashith. The early stages of the Cabala's evolution saw various names and attributes being applied to the Sephiroth. By the mid-thirteenth century the standard set of names had been settled, but a great deal of variation still exists among different Cabalistic traditions when it comes to the Names of God and other attributions that correspond to the Sephiroth.

The following names and attributions are standard in many branches of Western occultism:

Number: 1. *Name:* Kether. *Meaning:* Crown. *Astrological Attribution:* Primum Mobile.

Number: 2. *Name:* Chokmah. *Meaning:* Wisdom. *Astrological Attribution:* Sphere of Stars.

Number: 3. *Name:* Binah. *Meaning:* Understanding. *Astrological Attribution:* Saturn.

Number: 4. *Name:* Chesed. *Meaning:* Mercy. *Astrological Attribution:* Jupiter.

Number: 5. *Name:* Geburah. *Meaning:* Severity. *Astrological Attribution:* Mars.

Number: 6. *Name:* Tiphareth. *Meaning:* Beauty. *Astrological Attribution:* Sun.

Number: 7. *Name:* Netzach. *Meaning:* Victory. *Astrological Attribution:* Venus.

Number: 8. *Name:* Hod. *Meaning:* Glory. *Astrological Attribution:* Mercury.

Number: 9. *Name:* Yesod. *Meaning:* Foundation. *Astrological Attribution:* Moon.

Number: 10. *Name:* Malkuth. *Meaning:* Kingdom. *Astrological Attribution:* Earth.

In older Cabalistic writings, the Sephiroth are also called "sayings," "names," "lights," "powers," "crowns," "stages," "garments," "mirrors," and many other terms as well. They are also seen as the limbs or bodily parts of Adam Qadmon, the Primordial Human.

As this flurry of names suggests, the Sephiroth have many different aspects. Each Sephirah contains an entire Tree of Life within itself. As the old Cabalistic texts put it, each Sephirah "descends into itself," creating an infinity of realms and worlds inside itself. There are thus hidden worlds of mercy, justice, beauty, and so on, unfolding endlessly within each of the Sephiroth.

In the modern Hermetic and Pagan versions of the Cabala, the Sephiroth are often equated with the gods and goddesses of various Pagan religions. *SEE ALSO* CABALA; TREE OF LIFE.

Solomon: King of Israel, c. 986–c. 933 BCE. A son of David, the second king of Israel, by his favorite wife Bathsheba, Solomon ascended the throne on his father's death and reigned for forty years. His reign marked the high point of the Israelite kingdom, largely due to his father's successes, his own careful management of commerce and revenue, and the temporary weakness of Egypt and Babylonia, the great powers of the eastern Mediterranean area. With the assistance of his ally Hiram, king of Tyre, he built the first and most famous Temple of Jerusalem; *SEE* TEMPLE OF SOLOMON. In the last years of his reign, the expenses of his court, his building projects, and the maintenance of a large army created a rising current of unrest, and after his death a rebellion split the kingdom into the two states of Judah and Israel.

Biblical accounts of Solomon stress his wisdom and universal knowledge, and that reputation gradually spread to encompass the occult branches of knowledge. By Roman times, Solomon had acquired a reputation as the supreme master of magic; a bronze talismanic disk excavated from the Roman-era port at Ostia bears an image of him stirring an enchanter's cauldron with a long ladle. In the first century of the Common Era, the Jewish writer Josephus was already referring to books on the invocation of demons under Solomon's name.

In the Middle Ages and later, a large number of books of magic were attributed to him. The most famous of all the grimoires, the *Key of Solomon*, was credited to him, along with the *Lesser Key of Solomon*, or *Lemegeton*, the *Shemhamphorash of Solomon the King*, the *Testament of Solomon*, the *Book of the Throne of Solomon*, the *Book of Solomon on Gems and Spirits*, and many other occult titles, most of which did not escape the Christian church's strenuous attempts to find and burn them. *SEE* GRIMOIRE; LEMEGETON. Solomon was also considered in medieval times to be the founder of the Notory Art; *SEE* NOTORY ART.

It probably deserves to be mentioned that there is actually no evidence that Solomon himself had any involvement with magical practices at all, and his magical reputation is another example of the retrospective recruitment so common in occult history. *SEE* OCCULT HISTORY.

Star in the East, Order of the: An offshoot of Theosophy, the Order of the Star in the East was founded in 1911 as a vehicle for the claim that Jiddu Krishnamurti, the son of a servant at the Theosophical Society headquarters in Adyar, India, was the coming World Teacher of the New Age.

Heavily backed by Annie Besant and C. W. Leadbeater, at that time heads of the Theosophical Society, the order grew and flourished, reaching a total membership of well over 100,000. It was not entirely welcome to many old-line Theosophists, though and several groups – including most of the German section nf the society, led by its president Rudolph Steiner – split with the Theosophical Society over its championing of Krishnamurti and the order.

The order came to an abrupt halt in 1929 at the hands of Krishnamurti himself. Addressing a rally of order members, he proclaimed that "truth is a pathless land," denied that he was the World Teacher, and dissolved the order. This act of uncommon courage sent the Theosophical Society into a tailspin from which it has never really recovered. After the dissolution of the order, Krishnamurti went on to spend the rest of his life teaching and writing about his personal philosophy, which has little in common either with Theosophy or with the Western occult tradition.

Sun: One of the seven planets of traditional astrology, the sun in a birth chart represents the self, and in particular the public self—the face one shows to the world. In astrological terms, the sun rules the sign Leo, is exalted in Aries, is in his detriment in Aquarius and in his fall in Libra. *SEE* ASTROLOGY. In alchemy, the sun is a common symbol for gold, and also represents the *rubedo*, or red phase of the Great Work.

talisman: (Arabic *tilsam*, from Greek *tetelesmenon*, "that which has been consecrated") In magical lore, an object charged or consecrated with magical energies for the fulfillment of some specific purpose. Talismanic magic has had an important place in Western occultism since ancient times, and a dizzying variety of objects have been consecrated for various talismanic purposes.

Talismans can be traced in every magical tradition that has contributed to Western occultism. Ancient Egyptian priestly magicians had a wide range of talismanic methods at their disposal. For example, massive stone tablets were inscribed with healing spells and set in basins; those who were sick could pour water over the hieroglyphic carvings, drink the water, and benefit from the magic. More sinister rites were used to attack the foreign and domestic enemies of the Egyptian state; some of these made use of statues of enemy soldiers who were bound or maltreated and then buried in a secret place. *SEE* EGYPTIAN OCCULTISM.

Similar traditions could be found in the magical lore of the busy city-states of Mesopotamia, and the vast palace libraries of Ashurbanipal, the last great king of Assyria, include detailed instructions for a variety of talismanic magical workings. The magicians of Sumer, Babylon, and other Mesopotamian cultures drew heavily on the astrological lore of the region, setting a precedent that has been followed by talismanic magicians ever since.

Ancient Greece and Rome had a remarkable range of talisman lore, including the making of magical statues. A very common form of talismans was the binding tablet— a lead tablet that was dropped in wells, graves, caverns, and other points of ready access to the underworld to carry messages to the powers of the unseen and accomplish various forms of magic, usually hostile.

Talismans in the form now used in magic began to evolve toward the end of the classical period, with Egypt— where the art of writing had never quite lost its magical aura—as one focal point. The Graeco-Egyptian magical papyri, sorcerers' handbooks from the first few centuries of the Common Era, include instructions for making a variety of talismanic devices. It was after Egypt fell into Arab hands in the eighth century, though, that Muslim magicians began reshaping the lore they inherited from the ancient world, and evolved talismans of the sort that are still used today.

In this modern sense, a talisman is a piece of metal, paper, parchment, or some other material that can be engraved or written on. It is usually cut into a flat disk, although other shapes are known. Once made and marked with magically effective words and symbols, the talisman is consecrated in a formal ritual, and then concealed and left to do its work.

The methods used to consecrate a talisman vary widely in different traditions of magic. In medieval Arabic handbooks such as the *Picatrix*, and in many more recent works, the talisman is simply made of a metal with the right symbolism and held in the smoke of a specially compounded incense, then wrapped in silk and put away to work. The range of methods extends from this up to hugely complex techniques of the sort used by the Hermetic Order of the Golden Dawn, in which the magician can easily spend two hours reciting conjurations, vibrating divine names, evoking spirits, channeling energies, and putting the talisman through the equivalent of a lodge initiation ceremony. Both these approaches, and many that fall between these extremes, work well in practice.

Talismans, according to standard occult theory, work because their material basis forms a "body" for the energies placed in them at the time of consecration. With this anchor on the physical plane, the talisman keeps on working steadily and mindlessly toward the fulfillment of whatever purpose it was created to accomplish. When a talisman has finished its work, therefore, or when the situation has changed and its energies are no longer needed, it must be ceremonially deconsecrated and the physical form destroyed. While standard talismans of the type described above remain far and away the most common approach in use among ceremonial magicians, noticeably different approaches can be found among those who draw on folk magic traditions, especially those of American Hoodoo. In this system, a mojo, toby, or hand—that is, a small cloth bag filled with magically active substances— may be used for most of the purposes classical talismans might fill. Other traditions draw on various forms of natural magic to accomplish the same things; *SEE* NATURAL MAGIC.

Temple of Solomon: The most important building in Western occult symbolism, the Temple of Solomon was built in Jerusalem in the middle of the tenth century BCE. It was a rectangular building of stone, cedar, and gold, 60 cubits (about 103 feet) long, 20 cubits (around 34 feet) wide, and 30 cubits (around 52 feet) high. The entrance faced east, and was flanked by two brass pillars named Jachin ("stability") and Boaz ("strength"). Within was the sanctuary, 40 cubits long, and beyond that the Holy of Holies, the inner chamber in which the Ark of the Covenant and a few other sacred items were kept. The Holy of Holies was off limits to all but the High Priest himself, who entered it once a year.

The temple was destroyed in 586 BCE by the Assyrian Empire after an unsuccessful rebellion on the part of the Jews, and it remained in ruins for some seventy years, during which the Assyrian Empire gave way to a short-lived Babylonian Empire and much of the population of Israel was deported to Babylon. When the Babylonian Empire fell to the Persians, the new conquerors allowed the Jews to return home, and a new temple was built along the lines of the old. This was massively remodeled by Herod the Great, king of Judea, starting about 20 BCE, and destroyed down to the foundations in 70 CE by the Romans.

The detailed descriptions of the temple and its furnishings in the Old Testament (1 Kings 5:15–7:51 and 2 Chronicles 1:18–5:1) have prompted speculation, calculation, and fantasy for well over two thousand years. The medieval Knights Templar had their original headquarters on the site of the temple and took their name from it. The core mythology of Freemasonry centers on the building of the temple, and Masons whose enthusiasm exceeds their historical knowledge still sometimes claim that Masonry can trace its foundations to the time of Solomon; *SEE* FREE-MASONRY. The measurements and proportions of the temple, as described in the scriptural passages listed above, have also been heavily drawn on by students of the Cabala and sacred geometry from the Middle Ages onward. *SEE* CABALA; SACRED GEOMETRY. *SEE ALSO* SOLOMON.

Tetragrammaton: (Greek, "word of four letters") The most holy of the names of God in Cabala, as well as in the Jewish religion, the Tetragrammaton consists of the four letters Yod, Heh, Vau, Heh. Most modern scholars give its pronunciation as "Yahweh," while an older tradition with roots in the early Christian church transliterates it as "Jehovah" (which in classical Latin, the language in which this version was first written, is pronounced "Yehowah"). Many modern magicians "pronounce" it, even in ritual practice, simply by spelling it out letter by letter. Observant Jews do not pronounce it at all, and where it occurs in the scriptures, the name Adonai ("Lord") is read instead.

The word itself is probably an archaic form of the Hebrew verb "to be," and may mean something like "He Who Is." Especially in the old pronunciation "Yehowah," though, it bears a close resemblance to a whole family of names of gods and holy words in various ancient traditions—for example, the Roman title of Jupiter, Jove (in classical Latin, pronounced "Yoweh") or the Gnostic divine name IAO. The whole tradition may have its roots in the ancient use of vowel sequences as words of power.

In the Cabala, which has taken the Tetragrammaton as one of its major themes, an immense and complex symbolism has been developed out of it. The four Cabalistic worlds of Atziluth, Briah, Yetzirah, and Assiah each correspond to one of the letters of the Name, which has a special pronunciation in each world; this, in turn, gives rise to the secret name of the world. The letters of the Tetragrammaton are also rearranged by Cabalists into a total of twelve names of power, called the Twelve Banners of the Name, each of which corresponds to one of the twelve tribes of Israel, the twelve signs of the zodiac, and so forth. All these permutations have their magical uses. *SEE* CABALA.

theurgy: (Greek *theurgeia*, from *theos*, "god," and *ergeia*, "work") In ancient times, the magical wing of Platonism, which adopted ceremonial magic and traditional religious ritual as a process of purification needed to cleanse the lower aspects of the self and lay the foundation for the higher work of philosophical contemplation. Theurgy evolved as a distinct school in the first centuries of the Common Era, as part of the same fusion of Platonic philosophy and popular occultism that also brought about the creation of Hermeticism and many Gnostic traditions.

SEE GNOSTICISM; HERMETICISM. The major figure
in the formulation of theurgy was Iamblichus of Chalcis
(?–c. 330).

The theurgists led what was very nearly the last organized resistance against Christianity in the classical world.
Julian, the last Pagan emperor of Rome, was a committed
theurgist and a close student of Iamblichus' writings, and
the great resurgence of Pagan thought and practice in the
fourth century relied heavily on theurgy as both a philosophical stance and a basis for mutual toleration and support. Even after the political defeat of Paganism, theurgists such as Proclus and Sosipatra continued to teach and
practice. The tradition dwindled out slowly on the fringes
of the Byzantine Empire, and there is reason to believe
that it survived in outposts such as Harran until the Middle Ages.

The language of theurgy and some of its practices
were revived in the Renaissance in the wake of Marsilio
Ficino's epochal translation of the Hermetic treatises. *SEE*
CORPUS HERMETICUM. With the spread of knowledge
about classical Platonism and Hermeticism in the Renaissance, theurgy became an important element in the occult traditions of the time, and is discussed at length in
such classic Renaissance occult works as Heinrich Cornelius Agrippa's *Three Books of Occult Philosophy* (1531).

In recent usage, the term "theurgy" has come to refer to any form of magic that aims at the spiritual transformation of the magician—which, admittedly, was the primary goal of classical theurgy. *SEE* MAGIC. Several variant meanings also exist, however. In some French esoteric Christian systems, the word is used for a system of focused contemplative prayer that aims at practical as well as spiritual goals; *SEE* CHRISTIAN OCCULTISM. In some modern Pagan circles, it is used for any magical working that calls on the gods, as distinct from thaumaturgy, which uses the powers in natural substances or the magician himself or herself. *SEE ALSO* PLATONISM.

three: In Pythagorean number lore, three is the first actual number, since it has a beginning, a middle, and an end; one and two are considered to be basic principles of number rather than numbers in their own right. It represents two-dimensional space, since three points determine a plane. Its titles include "wisdom," "piety," and "friendship."

In the Cabala, three is Binah, Understanding, the third Sephirah of the Tree of Life. It is also the number of the letter Gimel. There are three mother letters in the Hebrew alphabet. Names of God containing three letters include ShDI, Shaddai, and I IUA, I Iu. *SEE* CABALA.

In Renaissance magical symbolism, three is the holiest and most powerful of numbers. It is the number of perfection and of ideal forms, and is associated with the Holy Trinity.

Tree of Life: In the Cabala, the arrangement formed by the ten Sephiroth and twenty-two Paths. The Tree of Life is the primary symbolic pattern of modern Western occultism, heavily used even by groups and traditions that claim no connection whatsoever to the Cabala.

The Tree of Life evolved gradually in Cabalistic circles in Spain and southern France out of discussions about the relation of the ten Sephiroth to one another. The essential arrangement of the Sephiroth was settled by the fourteenth century, but the relationship between the Sephiroth and the Paths remained open to debate for centuries thereafter, and there are still several different versions of the Tree in use at present, differing in the position and attributions of the Paths.

Various classifications of levels or stages within the Tree have been in circulation over the course of the Cabala's development. One very early division, discussed by the Spanish Cabalist Azriel of Gerona (fl. early thirteenth century), defines the topmost triangle of the Sephiroth as "intellectual," the next triangle as "mental," and the lowest triangle as "natural." (These terms are drawn from medieval metaphysics, and have caused a good deal of confusion in more recent times, since "intellect" in medieval thought meant roughly what "spiritual intuition" means nowadays.)

Another division, important in early writings but not much in evidence in the modern tradition, divided the Tree in half, with the upper five Sephiroth (Kether through Geburah) representing hidden powers and the lower five (Tiphareth through Malkuth) representing revealed powers. A somewhat similar division, more popular in recent writings, divides the three uppermost Sephiroth (the "Three Supernals") from the seven lower ones (the "Sephiroth of the Building"), which correspond to the seven days of the creation of the world in the Book of Genesis; between these is fixed a barrier, the Abyss.

Yet another division, much used in modern Cabala, divides the Tree according to the four worlds of the Cabala. In this system, the first Sephirah, Kether, belongs to the world of Atziluth; the second and third, Chokmah and Binah, belong to the world of Briah; the fourth through ninth belong to the world of Yetzirah; and the last, Malkuth, belongs to the world of Assiah. Alternatively, each of these worlds is often assigned a Tree of its own.

Also very important, throughout the history of Cabalistic thought, is the division of the Tree into three pillars. The right-hand pillar, comprising Chokmah, Chesed, and Netzach, is called the Pillar of Mercy or of Force. The left-hand pillar, comprising Binah, Geburah, and Hod, is called the Pillar of Severity or of Form. The central pillar, comprising Kether, Tiphareth, Yesod, and Malkuth, is called the Pillar of Mildness, Equilibrium, or Consciousness, or simply the Middle Pillar. The first two pillars are commonly associated with the two pillars of King Solomon's Temple, Jachin and Boaz. *SEE* BOAZ; JACHIN; TEMPLE OF SOLOMON.

In writings of the nineteenth- and twentieth-century magical renaissance, the Tree of Life is identified with the serpent Nehushtan and the upper astral, the realm of purification. *SEE* ASTRAL PLANE. *SEE ALSO* CABALA; SEPHIROTH.

vitriol: A fundamental term in alchemy with a wide range of meanings. In the most basic physical sense, vitriol is a term for several different hydrated metallic sulfate salts—copper sulfate ($CuSO_4$), or blue vitriol; iron sulfate ($FeSO_4$), or green vitriol; and zinc sulfate ($ZnSO_4$), or white vitriol—which are produced chemically by treating metals with sulfuric acid. As usual with alchemy, however, the term has also been given other meanings.

The word "vitriol" has also been used since medieval times as shorthand for the Latin phrase *Visita interiora terrae rectificando invenies occultum lapidem*, "Visit the interior of the earth, by rectifying you will find the hidden stone."

Voynich manuscript: Perhaps the most mysterious book in the world, this manuscript surfaced in 1912 in Frascati, Italy, in the bottom of an old chest at a Jesuit school. The American book dealer Wilfred Voynich bought it that same year, and brought it back to the United States. After passing through the hands of several owners, it was donated to Yale University in 1969.

The manuscript is a volume of 204 pages, six by nine inches in size, written in what is either a fiendishly difficult cipher or an unknown language. There were once another twenty-eight pages, but these are now lost. The writing looks like ordinary medieval script at first glance, but is actually in an alphabet of its own, one with twenty-nine letters, which has never been found in any other source. Along with the closely written text are little ink drawings in multiple colors, showing plants, astronomical constellations, and nude women in bathtubs.

With the manuscript was a letter dated August 19, 1666, from one Johannes Marcus Marci, rector of Prague University, to the famous Jesuit scholar and linguist Athanasius Kircher in Rome, explaining that the manuscript had been bought many years previously by Emperor Rudolf II for no less a sum than 600 ducats, and asking Kircher—an expert on codes—to try to make sense of it.

How it got to Prague remains a mystery, although there are clues that link the manuscript to a major figure in the Western esoteric tradition. Originally there were no page numbers in the manuscript, but someone made up that omission in the sixteenth century. The handwriting has been identified as that of John Dee, the great Elizabethan scholar and magician, who spent several years in Prague during the reign of Rudolf II. Clearly Dee had it in his possession at one point, and Dee's son Arthur Dee is on record as mentioning a book written entirely in "hieroglyphics" that his father had during his time in Prague. Whether Dee brought it with him from his home, where he had England's largest library, or whether it came to him in the course of his travels, is impossible to say.

There have been many different attempts at decoding the manuscript, and successful decipherments have been reported several times. Unfortunately none of these have succeeded in presenting a convincing case for their accuracy. Even an attempt by the National Security Agency to break the code with the aid of a Cray-6 supercomputer produced no useful result. It remains one of the major unsolved enigmas of our time.

Zohar: (Hebrew, "Splendor") The most important of all Cabalistic books, the Zohar is more a collection than a single treatise, comprising a series of separate tractates that fills five volumes in the standard printed editions. It presents itself as the recorded discussions of Simeon bar Yochai, an important Jewish mystical teacher of the second century CE, with his companions and friends. This attribution was accepted by most Cabalists up to recent times, and by the sixteenth century the legend had grown up that the Zohar as it now exists was a fragment of the original work, which had once been forty camel loads in size.

Linguistic and literary evidence, however, shows the Zohar to be a much more recent work, and all modern scholars agree that it was actually written by Moses de Leon (died 1305), a Jewish Cabalist who lived for most of his life in the small town of Guadalajara in Spain. It was composed in stages between 1270 and 1300, and most of it was in circulation by the time of its author's death. Vast, rambling, and diffuse, the Zohar is impossible to summarize and nearly as difficult to interpret. It assumes a very substantial background in Old Testament lore as well as Jewish legal, theological, philosophical, and mystical thought. Much of it consists of commentaries on scriptural verses, but these are interwoven with expositions on various parts of Cabalistic doctrine, narratives about the activities of Simeon bar Yochai and his companions, legendary stories, and a range of other material. Most of the themes and ideas of the traditional Jewish Cabala are covered in the course of the text.

The Zohar consists of a main portion, which is a Cabalistic commentary on the sections of the Torah read each week in Jewish worship, interspersed with several dozen shorter pieces on a dizzying array of subjects, from the creation of the universe to the practice of palmistry. Several of these latter may not have been written by Moses de Leon at all, but were composed by later writers and mistaken for portions of the Zohar. This sort of mistake was almost unavoidable because of the way the Zohar was "published." It was released by its author piecemeal, with the earliest parts going into circulation before 1281 (the date of the first quotation in another Cabalistic text) while other parts did not appear until at least a decade later. For several centuries manuscript collections of different parts of the Zohar were in circulation, and each Cabalist made do with whatever parts he was able to obtain. By the fifteenth century, complete manuscripts existed, and it was these that were used for the first printed versions, issued by competing Italian publishers in Mantua and Cremona in 1558–1560. The Zohar was originally written in Aramaic, the common language of Palestine during the second century CE, as part of Moses de Leon's attempt to present his views as those of Simeon bar Yochai. Important parts of the Zohar were translated into Latin by the French mystic Guillaume Postel and by the German occultist Christian Knorr von Rosenroth; the latter's work served as the basis for Samuel Mathers' English translation of three portions, first published in 1898 as *The Kabbalah Unveiled*, which has been a principal source of Zoharic lore for the English-speaking occult community ever since. *SEE ALSO* CABALA.

TO WRITE TO THE AUTHOR

If you wish to contact the author or would like more information about this book, please write to the author in care of Llewellyn Worldwide and we will forward your request. Both the author and publisher appreciate hearing from you and learning of your enjoyment of this book and how it has helped you. Llewellyn Worldwide cannot guarantee that every letter written to the author can be answered, but all will be forwarded. Please write to:

John Michael Greer
℅ Llewellyn Worldwide
2143 Wooddale Drive, 978-0-7387-2169-9
Woodbury, Minnesota 55125-2989, U.S.A.

Please enclose a self-addressed stamped envelope for reply, or $1.00 to cover costs. If outside U.S.A., enclose international postal reply coupon.